The Name Game: Forgotten Names of Legendary Rock Groups

Michael Pollick

Published by Michael Pollick, 2024.

While every precaution has been taken in the preparation of this book, the publisher assumes no responsibility for errors or omissions, or for damages resulting from the use of the information contained herein.

THE NAME GAME: FORGOTTEN NAMES OF LEGENDARY ROCK GROUPS

First edition. September 27, 2024.

Copyright © 2024 Michael Pollick.

ISBN: 979-8227603289

Written by Michael Pollick.

Table of Contents

The Name Game: Forgotten Names of Legendary Rock Groups

Michael Pollick

The Rolling Stones

You know, it's funny how names can stick with us, like that one friend who insists on calling you "Sparky" even though you haven't been a dog lover since you were five. Take, for instance, the legendary rock band The Rolling Stones. They've been shaking the world with their music for decades, but did you know they almost had a completely different name? Picture this: a bunch of scruffy guys from London, lounging around in a smoky pub, tossing around ideas for their band name. And what do they come up with? The Rollin' Stones. I mean, really? It sounds like a discount rock band that plays at your cousin's wedding. "Ladies and gentlemen, please welcome The Rollin' Stones! They'll be performing all your favorite hits, like 'You Can't Always Get What You Want' and 'I Can't Get No Satisfaction'—but only if you buy them a drink first!"

The name change was actually inspired by a Muddy Waters song, "Rollin' Stone." Suddenly, they went from sounding like a group of guys who might serenade you with a ukulele to a band that could rock your socks off. Imagine the world without "Paint It Black" or "Sympathy for the Devil." Instead, we'd be humming along to "I Can't Get No Satisfaction" while wondering if we should really be concerned about their rolling stone situation—like, do they need a rock doctor?

So, thank goodness they dropped the "g" and embraced their inner grit. The Rolling Stones became a symbol of rebellion, youth, and, let's be honest, a little bit of chaos. Who knew a simple name change could lead to a legacy? All hail the Stones, and may their name live on while we continue to roll on through life, one catchy tune at a time!

The Byrds

Imagine a world where The Byrds, those iconic purveyors of folk rock, were known by a name that sounds like a rejected title for a children's book. Yes, before they soared into the stratosphere of musical fame, they were originally called The Jet Set. Now, doesn't that sound like a group of hipsters who just learned how to use a travel app? Picture them, all decked out in mod suits, sipping on overpriced lattes, and discussing the merits of organic avocado toast while strumming their guitars. The Jet Set! It's the kind of name that makes you think they might be more interested in airport lounges than in making music that would define a generation.

But wait, it gets better! The name change came about in a rather amusing fashion. They realized that there was another band out there, also called The Jet Set, and they were probably just as confused about their own identity. So, in an effort to avoid a legal showdown that could rival a bad soap opera plot, they decided to rebrand themselves. And what did they come up with? The Byrds. Yes, Byrds, with a "y." Because nothing says "we're serious musicians" quite like a misspelled word that evokes images of chirping little creatures flitting about in the sunshine.

Now, you might think they pulled the name out of a hat, but there's actually a story behind it. They were inspired by the term "bird" as a slang for cool people. So, they took a leap of faith and embraced their inner avian. And thank goodness they did! Can you imagine if we were all singing "Jet Set" instead of "Mr. Tambourine Man"? It just doesn't have the same ring to it. So here's to The Byrds, the band that flew high with a name that didn't just take flight—it soared.

The Beatles

Imagine a world where the legendary band we know as The Beatles was actually called The Quarrymen. Yes, you heard that right! Before they became the Fab Four, they were just a bunch of teenagers jamming in Liverpool, trying to make sense of their mop-top haircuts and the burgeoning rock 'n' roll scene. The Quarrymen! It sounds like a group of stonemasons who decided to pick up guitars instead of chisels. Picture John Lennon with a hard hat and Paul McCartney wielding a pickaxe instead of a bass guitar. I mean, can you really picture them belting out "Hey Jude" while wearing safety goggles?

The name itself comes from the Quarry Bank High School where some of the band members met, which is a bit like naming a band after your high school cafeteria. "Hey, let's call ourselves The Lunchroom Legends!" It's endearing, but it doesn't exactly scream rock stardom. Yet, as fate would have it, they eventually decided that being named after a school was as cool as a pair of socks with sandals.

So, they transformed into The Beatles, a name that not only rolls off the tongue but also plays a clever pun on the word "beat," as in the rhythm of their music. Plus, who wouldn't want to be associated with the idea of cute, fuzzy insects? It's like they took a giant leap from the Quarrymen to The Beatles, and suddenly they were in a whole new league—one where they could wear matching suits, sport bowl cuts, and charm the world with their harmonies.

So next time you listen to "Twist and Shout," just remember: it could have been "Chisel and Shout." And thank your lucky stars that they chose to rock instead of quarry!

Alice Cooper

You know, when you think of Alice Cooper, you probably picture wild stage antics, outrageous costumes, and a voice that can send shivers down your spine. But let's rewind a bit to the origins of this iconic band, back when they were known as... wait for it... The Spiders. Yes, The Spiders! Can you imagine? A bunch of long-haired rockers strutting around with that name? I mean, it's like calling a heavy metal band "The Fluffy Kittens." It just doesn't have the same bite, does it?

Now, The Spiders had their fair share of challenges. For starters, they were competing with a lot of other bands with equally ridiculous names. Picture it: "The Spiders" on the same bill as "The Electric Prunes" and "The Velvet Underground." It's like a battle of the bizarre! But the name game didn't stop there. They eventually transformed into "Alice Cooper," which, believe it or not, was the name of a fictional character they created. I can just imagine them sitting around, brainstorming names, and someone says, "How about Alice? And let's throw in Cooper for good measure!" It's like naming a pet goldfish "Darth Vader."

But here's the kicker: they didn't even realize that Alice Cooper was actually a name that a lot of people associated with a sweet, innocent girl. It's like they took the most wholesome name they could find and turned it into a symbol of shock rock! Talk about a plot twist. So, the next time you're headbanging to "School's Out," just remember that it all started with a bunch of guys who thought they could scare the world with a name that sounded like a character from a children's book. And honestly, isn't that just rock and roll in a nutshell?

Pearl Jam

You know, it's funny how names can stick with us, like that one embarrassing nickname from high school that you just can't shake off. Take Pearl Jam, for instance. We all know them as the grunge legends who brought us anthems of angst and rebellion, but did you know they almost went by a completely different name? That's right! Before they were rocking out stadiums and selling millions of albums, they were known as Mookie Blaylock. Yes, you heard that correctly. Mookie Blaylock! Now, if you're scratching your head wondering who on earth that is, let me enlighten you. Mookie Blaylock was actually a professional basketball player in the '90s, known for his impressive skills on the court and, let's be honest, a name that sounds like a character from a cartoon.

Imagine walking into a record store in 1991 and asking for the latest Mookie Blaylock album. The clerk would probably look at you like you just asked for a vinyl of cat meows. The band eventually decided that maybe, just maybe, naming themselves after a basketball player wasn't the best marketing strategy. I mean, it's hard to rock out when people are still trying to figure out if you're a band or a sports team! So, they settled on Pearl Jam, a name that conjures images of ocean waves and, well, jam. But here's the kicker: the name "Pearl Jam" is rumored to be inspired by a family recipe for jam made by Eddie Vedder's great-grandmother, who may or may not have had a thing for pearls.

So, next time you're jamming out to "Alive," just remember, it could have been a lot more confusing. "Hey, have you heard the new Mookie Blaylock track?" Yeah, I'll stick with Pearl Jam, thanks!

Led Zeppelin

You know, there's something fascinating about rock band names. They often reflect a certain attitude, a rebellious spirit, or even a clever pun. Take Led Zeppelin, for instance. Now, before they became the legendary rock gods we know today, they were almost known by a rather peculiar name: "Lead Zeppelin." Yes, you heard that right. Imagine if they'd stuck with that! It sounds like a failed science project or a new kind of airship that never took off—literally!

The story goes that the band was formed after Jimmy Page, the guitarist, brought together a bunch of musicians, including Robert Plant and John Bonham. They were jamming and cooking up some serious rock magic when someone joked that their sound would go down like a "lead balloon." Now, if you're not familiar with British slang, that means it would crash and burn spectacularly. But instead of taking it as a warning, they decided to embrace the name. They thought it was funny, and honestly, who wouldn't want to be associated with a balloon that's heavy enough to sink?

But here's where it gets even better: the spelling! They changed "Lead" to "Led" because they thought it would look cooler and also to avoid confusion. After all, who wants to be known as the band that can't spell? It's like naming your band "The Great Spelling Bee" and then failing to spell "bee" correctly.

So, there you have it. From a joke about a balloon that's too heavy to fly to one of the most iconic names in rock history, Led Zeppelin is a testament to how a little humor and a lot of creativity can lead to something monumental. Just remember, if you ever hear someone mention "Lead Zeppelin," you can chuckle and say, "You mean the band that almost sank before they even took off?"

Motley Crue

So, let's talk about one of the most iconic rock bands of all time: Mötley Crüe. You know, the guys who practically defined glam metal, with their wild hair, leather, and enough eyeliner to make a raccoon jealous. But did you know that before they were known as Mötley Crüe, they had a name that sounds like it was pulled from a toddler's attempt to name a pet? Yes, I'm talking about the original name: "Christmas." Yes, you heard that right! Christmas! Can you imagine? The band that brought us "Girls, Girls, Girls" and "Kickstart My Heart" started off with a name that evokes visions of jingle bells and fruitcake.

Picture it: Vince Neil, Nikki Sixx, Tommy Lee, and Mick Mars, all decked out in spandex and glitter, but instead of roaring guitars, they're belting out carols. "Jingle Bells" with a heavy metal twist, anyone? "Dashing through the snow, in a one-horse open sleigh... with a bottle of Jack and a head full of dreams!"

But here's the kicker. The name "Christmas" was actually a joke. It was originally a way to poke fun at the band's own chaotic nature. I mean, it's hard to take a group seriously when their name sounds like a holiday party gone wrong. It wasn't long before they realized that if they wanted to make it big, they needed something a bit more edgy. Enter "Mötley Crüe," a name that sounds like it should be stamped on a leather jacket or a tattoo.

So, next time you're headbanging to "Dr. Feelgood," just remember that it could have been "Jingle Bells" instead. And who knows, maybe they'd have made it a holiday classic, complete with an accompanying music video featuring Santa and his sleigh! Now that's a Christmas special I'd pay to see.

The B-52s

So, let's talk about the B-52s, the iconic band that brought us "Rock Lobster" and "Love Shack." You might think their name is just a quirky nod to a funky airplane or a cool hairstyle, but oh, my friends, it's so much more than that. Picture this: it's the late 1970s in Athens, Georgia, a town buzzing with art, music, and a whole lot of weirdness. A group of friends decides to form a band, and they need a name. They brainstorm, and someone, probably after a few too many cocktails, throws out "The B-52s."

Now, here's the kicker: the name actually comes from a type of beehive hairdo that was all the rage back then, reminiscent of the B-52 bomber, which is a plane that could drop some serious bombs, both literally and metaphorically. It's like saying, "Hey, we're going to blow you away with our music, but first, let's make sure our hair is taller than our amps!" Imagine the scene: a bunch of hipsters in outrageous outfits, sporting towering hairstyles that could double as Wi-Fi hotspots, all while debating the merits of their name.

But wait, it gets better! Before they settled on "B-52s," they toyed with names like "The Four Sassy Cats" and "The Martian Dancers." Can you imagine? "Ladies and gentlemen, put your hands together for The Martian Dancers!" It sounds like an intergalactic circus act.

In the end, they went with the B-52s, and thank goodness for that! Because who wouldn't want to dance to the sounds of a band named after a hairstyle that could survive a hurricane? So, here's to the B-52s, proving that sometimes, the best names come from the wildest ideas and the tallest hairdos!

AC/DC

I magine a world where rock legends never quite made it to the stage, where the electrifying riffs of AC/DC were instead delivered by a band called "Geordie's Revenge." Yes, you heard that right! Before the iconic name that has become synonymous with high-voltage rock 'n' roll, the band almost went by a title that sounds more like a local pub brawl than a global phenomenon.

Picture the scene: a group of scrappy musicians huddled in a dimly lit garage, brainstorming names. "Geordie's Revenge" was a nod to their roots, evoking images of a band fueled by the spirit of Newcastle. But let's be honest, who wants to rock out to a name that sounds like a bad sequel to a medieval drama? "And now, ladies and gentlemen, please welcome... Geordie's Revenge!" Cue the crickets.

Then, like a lightning bolt out of the blue, someone suggested "AC/DC." The name, derived from the electrical terminology meaning "alternating current/direct current," was a stroke of genius. It perfectly captured the band's electrifying energy and raw power. It's like they knew they were about to unleash a sonic storm upon the world.

Can you imagine the confusion if they had stuck with "Geordie's Revenge"? Concertgoers would be scratching their heads, wondering if they accidentally wandered into a folk festival instead of a rock show. "What's next? A band called 'Tea and Crumpets'?"

So, here we are, celebrating the genius of a name change that saved us from the musical equivalent of a soggy biscuit. AC/DC became a household name, while "Geordie's Revenge" remains a humorous footnote in rock history, a reminder that sometimes, it's the name that can make or break the sound. Rock on!

Van Halen

Imagine a world where the legendary rock band Van Halen wasn't called Van Halen at all. Picture this: a group of scrappy musicians in the 1970s, fueled by dreams of fame and a love for loud guitars, sitting around trying to come up with the perfect name. They could have gone with something like "The Mighty Munchkins" or "The Flying Tofu." Yes, you heard that right! Before they settled on the name that would become synonymous with rock and roll, they toyed with "Genesis." But hold your horses! That name was already taken by a certain British band that wasn't exactly keen on sharing their thunder.

So, they turned to their own roots. The band was originally called "Mammoth." Now, that's a name that really packs a punch, doesn't it? But let's be honest, it sounds more like a circus act than a rock band. "Ladies and gentlemen, welcome to the stage... Mammoth!" You can almost hear the crickets chirping. The name conjures images of oversized, furry creatures lumbering around, not of electrifying guitar solos and wild stage antics.

Then, out of the blue, they had a lightbulb moment. They realized they could simply slap their last name on the marquee. "Van Halen" rolled off the tongue, and boom! They were ready to take the world by storm. It's catchy, it's memorable, and it's a whole lot better than "Mammoth." Imagine trying to explain the band to your friends: "Hey, have you heard that new song by Mammoth?" You'd get a lot of confused looks. So, here's to Van Halen, a name that truly rocks, and to the near-miss that could have left us all scratching our heads, wondering what on earth a Mammoth concert would look like!

Nirvana

Imagine a world where one of the most iconic rock bands of the 90s was not called Nirvana, but rather... "Pen Cap Chew." Yes, you heard that right. Before they became the grunge legends we know today, Kurt Cobain and his bandmates had a name that sounds more like a quirky art project than a musical powerhouse. I mean, can you picture it? "Hey, did you catch the latest Pen Cap Chew album?" It just doesn't have the same ring to it, does it?

The story goes that Cobain wanted something that captured the essence of their sound, something that felt raw and real. But "Pen Cap Chew" was a name born out of a moment of whimsy, a name that evokes images of a bored student chewing on a pen cap during a particularly dull lecture. It's almost as if they were trying to make a statement about the mundanity of life, or perhaps they just hadn't had their coffee yet.

This name change happened in 1988, and thank goodness for that! Can you imagine the confusion at a concert? "Ladies and gentlemen, please welcome to the stage... Pen Cap Chew!" The audience would probably be looking around, wondering if they had accidentally wandered into an avant-garde performance art piece instead of a rock concert.

Nirvana, on the other hand, evokes images of bliss, transcendence, and an escape from the everyday grind. It's a name that resonates with the spirit of rebellion and the quest for something greater. So, let's raise a toast to the moment when Cobain decided to ditch the pen cap and embrace the idea of Nirvana, because without that leap of faith, we might have been stuck in a world where "Smells Like Teen Spirit" was performed by a band with a name that sounds more like a dental hygiene campaign.

Queen

You know, it's funny to think about how the legendary rock band Queen almost had a completely different name. Picture this: a world where Freddie Mercury, with his flamboyant stage presence and powerful vocals, is belting out hits under the banner of... wait for it... "Smile." Yes, you heard me right! Before they became the iconic band we know today, they were known as Smile. Now, I don't know about you, but "Smile" sounds more like a dental hygiene campaign than a rock band, doesn't it? "Brush twice a day and rock out with Smile!"

The original lineup included Freddie Mercury's future bandmates, Brian May and Roger Taylor, and they were all about that sweet, sweet rock sound. But let's be real; "Smile" lacks the punch of "Queen." It's like a gentle nudge instead of a full-on rock explosion. Imagine walking into a concert and hearing, "Ladies and gentlemen, please welcome to the stage... Smile!" The crowd would probably just nod politely and sip their drinks, wondering if they'd accidentally wandered into a therapy session.

Now, Freddie, being the visionary he was, decided that "Smile" just didn't cut it. He wanted something bold, something that would make an impact. And boy, did he hit the jackpot with "Queen." It's regal, it's powerful, and it's got that perfect mix of glam and grit. It's like he took a look at the name "Smile" and thought, "Nope, we need to be more fabulous!"

So, next time you're singing along to "Bohemian Rhapsody," just take a moment to appreciate that it could have been "Bohemian

Toothpaste" if things had gone differently. Thank you, Freddie, for giving us Queen and sparing us from a lifetime of dental rock!

The Guess Who

You know, it's funny how names can stick to you like gum on a shoe, and the rock band The Guess Who is no exception. Before they became the iconic Canadian rockers we know today, they were originally known as Chad Allan and the Expressions. I mean, can you imagine? "Chad Allan and the Expressions." It sounds like the name of a high school jazz band that only plays at prom. "Hey, did you catch Chad Allan and the Expressions last night? They really nailed that rendition of 'Dancing Queen!'" Not quite the same vibe as "The Guess Who," right?

So, how did they go from Chad Allan and the Expressions to The Guess Who? Well, it all started with a little bit of mischief. The band was playing a gig, and someone in the audience shouted, "Who are you?" In a moment of sheer genius—or perhaps sheer desperation—they decided to roll with it. They responded, "Guess who?" and just like that, a legend was born. Talk about a branding strategy! Forget focus groups and market research; sometimes, all you need is a cheeky audience member and a quick wit.

And let's be real, "The Guess Who" is much more intriguing. It leaves you with a sense of mystery, like a musical game of hide-and-seek. "Guess who's coming to dinner? Oh, it's just The Guess Who!" It's a conversation starter, a playful jab at your curiosity. Plus, it's way easier to fit on a T-shirt than "Chad Allan and the Expressions." Imagine trying to explain that name at a concert: "Yeah, I'm here to see Chad Allan and the... uh... what was it again?"

So, hats off to that cheeky audience member who turned a band's fate around with a simple question. Who knew a little whimsy could lead to rock 'n' roll history?

Creedence Clearwater Revival

You know, there's something absolutely hilarious about the original name of the legendary rock band Creedence Clearwater Revival. I mean, when you think of Creedence Clearwater Revival, you picture a group of long-haired musicians belting out tunes that make you want to drive down a winding road with the windows down, right? But here's the kicker: they almost went by the name "The Golliwogs." Yes, you heard that right! The Golliwogs! It sounds like a band of cartoon characters, maybe a group of animated marshmallows trying to make it big in the music scene. Can you imagine? "Hey, have you heard the new single from The Golliwogs?" It's like a bad joke waiting to happen.

Now, you might wonder where that name even came from. Well, it turns out it was inspired by a children's book character, but by the time they were ready to hit the big time, the name had become a bit... shall we say, problematic? You see, "golliwog" has some pretty controversial associations. So, in a brilliant stroke of marketing genius, they decided to ditch the name and rebrand themselves as Creedence Clearwater Revival. Talk about a glow-up! Suddenly, they went from sounding like a band that would play at your grandma's tea party to one that would rock out at a festival.

The new name not only had a catchy ring to it but also evoked images of nature and freedom. It was like they were saying, "We're here to save rock and roll!" And save it they did, with hits that still echo through the airwaves today. So next time you crank up "Bad Moon Rising," just remember: it could have been "The Golliwogs." Thank goodness for creative rebranding, right?

The Band

You know, it's funny how names can stick, especially in the world of rock and roll. Take The Band, for instance. You might think, "Wow, what a clever name!" But let me take you back to their original moniker: The Hawks. Yes, The Hawks! Can you imagine if they'd stuck with that? Picture it: "Ladies and gentlemen, please welcome to the stage… The Hawks!" Sounds like a minor league baseball team, doesn't it? "Brought to you by your local car dealership, The Hawks are here to knock it out of the park!"

Now, The Hawks were no ordinary band. They were the backing group for the legendary Bob Dylan, and let's be real, you can't just be a backing band with a name like The Hawks and expect to be taken seriously. I mean, what's next? The Sparrows? The Pigeons? "Hey, we're The Pigeons, and we're here to coo our way into your hearts!"

So, when they decided to drop the bird-themed name for something a bit more enigmatic, it was a stroke of genius. "The Band" sounds like a collective of musical geniuses, right? It's like they're saying, "Forget the individual members; we are the essence of music itself!"

And let's not overlook the irony. They became one of the most iconic bands in history, and yet, their name is so bland it could be the title of a corporate seminar. "Join us for The Band: Strategies for Effective Collaboration!"

So here's to The Band, the band that was once The Hawks. They soared to greatness, proving that sometimes, it's not about the name you choose but the music you create. Just imagine if they hadn't made the change; we'd all be singing "The Weight" while wearing baseball caps!

The Kinks

You know, it's funny how names can shape our perceptions, right? Take, for instance, the legendary rock band The Kinks. We all know them for their catchy tunes and that unmistakable British flair, but did you know they almost went by a completely different name? That's right! Before they became the iconic Kinks, they were originally called The Ray Davies Quartet. Now, I don't know about you, but that sounds more like a group of jazz musicians who might serenade you at a coffee shop rather than rock legends who would later give us hits like "You Really Got Me."

Imagine it: "Hey, did you catch The Ray Davies Quartet last night?" I mean, it doesn't exactly inspire visions of wild guitar riffs and headbanging, does it? It sounds more like a polite gathering of chaps discussing the finer points of tea brewing. And let's be honest, "The Ray Davies Quartet" doesn't quite scream "rebellious rock band." It's like calling a bulldog "Fluffy." You just know something's off.

But here's where it gets even better. The name change happened partly because they were tired of being mistaken for a jazz group. I can just picture them in a smoky club, trying to play their music while someone yells, "Hey, when's the sax solo coming?" So, they needed a name that would make people sit up and take notice. Enter "The Kinks." It's punchy, it's quirky, and it's unforgettable. Plus, it gave them the perfect excuse for their wild stage antics.

So, the next time you hear "You Really Got Me" blasting through your speakers, just remember: it could have been The Ray Davies Quartet, and we'd all be a little worse off for it!

R.E.M.

Imagine, if you will, a world where the iconic rock band R.E.M. was known by a name that sounds more like a sleep disorder than a musical phenomenon. Yes, before they graced our ears with unforgettable hits, they were once called "Twisted Kites." I mean, really? Twisted Kites? It conjures up images of a bunch of college kids tangled in string, frantically trying to untangle their dreams while the wind laughs at their misfortunes.

Picture Michael Stipe, the enigmatic frontman, standing on stage, passionately belting out "Losing My Religion" while wearing a shirt that says "Twisted Kites." It's hard to imagine the same band that gave us such profound, introspective lyrics also had a name that sounds like a failed art project. It's as if they were trying to evoke the carefree spirit of childhood while simultaneously reminding us that sometimes, life just doesn't fly as high as we hope.

But the story gets better. The name change came about because, let's be honest, "Twisted Kites" might not have been the best choice for a band aiming for international fame. It's hard to be taken seriously when your name sounds like a bad metaphor for emotional baggage. So, they went for something more abstract, something that could evoke curiosity and intrigue. And thus, R.E.M. was born, a name that stands for "Rapid Eye Movement," a nod to the mysterious nature of dreams and the subconscious.

So, next time you find yourself humming "Everybody Hurts," just remember that it could have been "Everybody's Got Twisted Kites." Who knows? Maybe they would have become the poster band for kite enthusiasts everywhere, or perhaps they'd be the soundtrack to a quirky indie film about flying kites. Either way, I think we can all agree that R.E.M. was a much better choice.

Heart

You know, it's funny how names can shape our perceptions. Take the rock band Heart, for instance. When you hear "Heart," you might think of soaring ballads and powerful vocals, but let's rewind to their original name: "The Army." Yes, you heard that right. The Army. It's like they were trying to recruit fans for a rock and roll draft, and I can just imagine their promotional posters: "Join The Army! No basic training required, just a love for electric guitars and a penchant for leather pants!"

Now, you might wonder how they went from a military-themed title to something that evokes feelings of love and emotion. Well, the story goes that the band was formed in the early 1970s, and let's face it, they probably realized that "The Army" wasn't exactly the most appealing name for a group of glam rockers. I mean, who wants to be associated with boot camp when you could be belting out "Barracuda"? So, they decided to make a change, and thus, Heart was born. It's a name that flows, a name that beats—pun intended.

But here's the kicker: think about the confusion at the time. Imagine fans showing up at a gig, only to find out they weren't about to enlist but rather enjoy some hard-hitting rock music. "I thought I was joining The Army, not watching a power ballad concert!" They must have felt like they'd been drafted into an entirely different kind of battle—one filled with glitter and high notes instead of drills and push-ups.

So, the next time you listen to Heart, just remember: they could have been The Army, but thankfully, they chose to go for a name that truly resonates. And who knows? Maybe their first album would have been titled "Boot Camp Blues."

Genesis

You know, it's funny how names can stick with you, like that one friend who refuses to stop calling you "Squeaky" even after you've grown out of your childhood phase. Take the legendary rock band Genesis, for instance. When you hear "Genesis," you might think of the beginning of something grand, a biblical reference, or perhaps a video game console from the '90s. But did you know that before they became the iconic band we know today, they were called "The Garden Wall"? Yes, you heard that right! The Garden Wall. It sounds less like a rock band and more like a quaint little gardening club where members discuss the best types of mulch over herbal tea.

Imagine the band members sitting around, strumming their guitars, and saying, "Hey, let's rock out under the name of a garden feature!" It's a name that conjures images of flower arrangements and hedge trimming rather than electric guitars and drum solos. I can just picture them trying to book gigs: "Hi, we're The Garden Wall. We play progressive rock!" and the venue manager scratching his head, wondering if he should set up a flower stand.

But then, in a stroke of genius—or perhaps desperation—they changed their name to Genesis. Suddenly, they went from sounding like a group of horticulturists to the pioneers of rock music. It's like swapping out your mom's minivan for a sleek sports car. The name Genesis implied a rebirth, a fresh start, and it fit perfectly with their ambitious sound. So, the next time you crank up "Invisible Touch," just remember: it could have been "The Garden Wall" serenading you instead. And let's be honest, that's a concert no one would want to attend!

Journey

You know, when you think of the band Journey, you probably picture soaring vocals, epic guitar solos, and a soundtrack to every high school dance from the '80s. But did you know that this legendary band almost had a name that sounded more like a bad sci-fi movie than a rock group? That's right! Before they became the iconic Journey we know and love, they were originally called "The Golden Gate Rhythm Section." I mean, come on! It sounds like a jazz band that plays at your uncle's retirement party, not a rock band that would eventually give us "Don't Stop Believin.'"

Can you imagine? "The Golden Gate Rhythm Section" rolling onto the stage, decked out in polyester suits, trying to get the crowd pumped up with a name that sounds like it belongs in a tourist brochure. "Hey folks, come see The Golden Gate Rhythm Section! We'll take you on a musical journey through the fog of San Francisco!" I can picture it: fans scratching their heads, wondering if they should bring a picnic basket or a dance partner.

But here's the kicker: the band members realized that this name just wasn't going to cut it. They needed something that resonated, something that captured the spirit of their music. So, they went through a brainstorming session that must have looked like a bunch of dudes sitting around with their guitars, tossing out names like they were playing a bizarre game of rock 'n' roll charades.

Eventually, they settled on "Journey," which sounds way cooler and a whole lot more adventurous. I mean, who wouldn't want to go on a journey? Just remember, if it weren't for a few creative minds and a whole lot of laughter, we might be belting out "Don't Stop Believin'" while pretending to dance to "The Golden Gate Rhythm Section." Now that's a journey I'm glad we avoided!

Aerosmith

So, let's take a moment to dive into the fascinating, slightly ridiculous world of rock band names, specifically Aerosmith. Now, you may know them as the legendary purveyors of rock anthems and power ballads, but did you know they almost had a name that sounds like a rejected brand of cough syrup? Yes, before they became the iconic Aerosmith, they were known as... wait for it... "The Jam Band." I mean, really? The Jam Band? It sounds like a group of musicians who couldn't decide between a fruit spread or a rock concert!

Picture this: a bunch of long-haired rockers in the '70s, strutting around with their denim jackets, and the only thing they can come up with is "The Jam Band." It's like naming a dog "Dog." You know, it's functional, but it lacks flair. They might as well have called themselves "The Band That Plays Music."

But it gets better! They eventually settled on Aerosmith, which, let's be honest, sounds like a superhero whose power is to create wind with a guitar riff. The name conjures images of soaring through the skies, hair blowing in the wind, playing epic solos while saving the world from bad music.

Now, the origin of the name? It was inspired by a combination of the word "aero" meaning air and "smith," which evokes craftsmanship. So, while "The Jam Band" might have left us wondering if we should bring crackers, Aerosmith gives us the sense of an airborne rock experience, a little bit of artistry mixed with a whole lot of attitude.

In the end, thank goodness they ditched the jam for a little more rock 'n' roll. Who knows? If they hadn't, we might have been stuck with "The Jam Band" on our playlists, and let's be real—no one wants to rock out to that!

KISS

You know, there's a little nugget of rock history that I find absolutely hilarious, and it involves one of the most iconic bands of all time: KISS. Now, we all know KISS for their outrageous costumes, face paint, and, of course, that unforgettable anthem "Rock and Roll All Nite." But did you know that before they became the legendary KISS, they were almost called... wait for it... "Wicked Lester"? Yes, you heard me right—Wicked Lester! It sounds like the name of a bad magician who can't quite pull off a card trick, doesn't it? "Ladies and gentlemen, prepare to be amazed by Wicked Lester, the man who can make your hopes disappear!"

Imagine if they had stuck with that name. "Hey, do you want to go see Wicked Lester in concert?" It just doesn't have the same ring to it, does it? I can picture it now—Gene Simmons, with his fire-breathing antics, dressed as a wizard, waving a wand instead of his signature bass guitar. And Paul Stanley, the Starchild, probably would have been wearing a pointy hat instead of that iconic star makeup. It's hard to believe that this band, known for their hard rock and rebellious spirit, almost went for a name that sounds like a rejected character from a children's book.

But, in a twist of fate, they transformed into KISS, which, depending on who you ask, either stands for "Knights in Satan's Service" or "Kids in Satan's Service." Honestly, I think it just stands for "Keep It Simple, Stupid," because that's what rock and roll is all about! So, next time you're rocking out to "Detroit Rock City," just remember: it could have been "Wicked Lester," and we'd be living in a very different world of rock music, one where the biggest hit might've been "Abracadabra, I'm Outta Here!"

Black Sabbath

You know, it's funny how names can shape our perceptions. Take Black Sabbath, for instance. When you hear that name, you probably think of dark, heavy riffs, haunting lyrics, and a certain sense of doom that makes you want to headbang while contemplating your life choices. But did you know that the band almost had a completely different name? That's right! Before they became the iconic heavy metal giants we know today, they went by the name Earth. Earth! I mean, come on! It sounds like a name for a nature documentary or a particularly boring environmental club meeting. "Join Earth! We plant trees and discuss composting!"

The story goes that they were playing gigs under this name, trying to make a name for themselves, but there was a problem. They were too heavy for the name Earth. I can just picture it: a bunch of leather-clad rockers on stage, screaming about the end of the world while the audience thinks they're there for a seminar on recycling. Talk about a mismatch!

Eventually, they realized that their sound was evolving, and they needed something that matched their vibe. So, they took inspiration from a horror movie. They saw a film called "Black Sabbath," and the rest is history. Suddenly, they went from being Earth to Black Sabbath, and with that change, they unleashed a whole new world of music.

Imagine if they had stuck with Earth. We'd have "Earth Day" concerts instead of heavy metal festivals. The album covers would feature trees instead of skulls, and their lyrics would probably be about saving the planet instead of the existential dread that makes metal so appealing. So, here's to Black Sabbath and their brilliant rebranding! Who knew a name could rock so hard?

Metallica

You know, it's funny how history has a way of twisting the narratives we think we know. Take Metallica, for example. The name that conjures images of headbanging teens, leather jackets, and guitar solos that could wake the dead. But did you know their original name was... wait for it... "Mettallica"? Yes, that's right! With two T's, because why not? It's like they were trying to be the world's most intense spelling bee champions. "Mettallica, can you use it in a sentence?" "Sure! We're a band that plays heavy metal music, and we might just melt your face off!"

But here's where it gets even better. The name "Mettallica" was actually inspired by a friend of drummer Lars Ulrich, who was running a magazine called Metallica. Lars thought, "Hey, that's a cool name! Let's just take it and run!" It's like borrowing your friend's favorite hoodie and never giving it back. "Oh, you don't mind, do you? I'll just wear it on stage in front of thousands of people."

Then, as fate would have it, they discovered that spelling it with one T made it look and sound way cooler. It's like they were trying to find the perfect balance between heavy metal and a spelling error. So they dropped a T, and voila! Metallica was born.

Can you imagine if they had stuck with "Mettallica"? I can just see it now: a bunch of leather-clad fans yelling, "Mettallica! Mettallica!" It sounds more like a weird Italian dish than a legendary rock band. "I'll have the Mettallica with a side of headbanging, please!" But here we are, and the rest is history. They went from a spelling mistake to one of the biggest names in rock. Who knew a single T could make such a difference?

Matchbox 20

You know, I always thought the name "Matchbox 20" was a cool, edgy name for a rock band. It has that whole mysterious vibe, like you're about to uncover some deep, dark secret. But here's the kicker: they almost went with a name that sounds like it was plucked straight from a middle school art project. Yes, folks, before they became the iconic band we know today, they were originally called "Tabitha's Secret." I mean, come on! Tabitha's Secret? It sounds less like a rock band and more like a quirky children's book about a cat who can't stop telling secrets.

Picture this: a smoky bar, the crowd buzzing with anticipation, and then the lead singer steps up to the mic and says, "Hey everyone, we're Tabitha's Secret!" Cue the crickets. You could almost hear the collective confusion as people wondered if they were about to hear a ballad about a lost kitten or a power anthem about, I don't know, the importance of sharing secrets.

But here's where it gets even better. The band members realized that the name didn't quite capture the essence of their sound. They needed something that screamed "we're here to rock your socks off!" So, they pivoted to "Matchbox 20," which sounds like a secret society of musicians who meet in a basement to discuss the finer points of songwriting while drinking lukewarm soda.

In the end, thank goodness they made the switch. I can't imagine belting out "Push" or "3AM" with a name like Tabitha's Secret. I mean, who would take them seriously? So here's to Matchbox 20, a name that's not just catchy but also a reminder that sometimes, you have to burn the script and start fresh—preferably with a name that doesn't sound like a children's TV show.

Goo Goo Dolls

Ah, the Goo Goo Dolls, a name that evokes images of catchy melodies and heartfelt ballads, but let's rewind the tape a bit, shall we? Before they were serenading us with "Iris" and "Slide," they were known as the most bizarrely named band you could imagine: the Sex Maggots. Yes, you heard that right—the Sex Maggots. It sounds like a punk band that would play in a dingy basement somewhere, and honestly, it's a name that would make your grandmother clutch her pearls and question her parenting choices.

Now, picture this: a group of scruffy musicians in the late '80s, jamming out in Buffalo, New York, with a name like that. I mean, how do you even introduce yourself? "Hey, we're the Sex Maggots, and this is our new single!" It's like they were daring every venue owner to kick them out before they even set foot on stage. But let's be real, the name was probably a tongue-in-cheek nod to the punk scene of the time, where shock value was king, and anything less would get you laughed out of the garage.

But as they started to gain traction and realized that maybe, just maybe, they wanted to reach a wider audience than just the grimy corners of the underground scene, they decided to change their name. Enter the Goo Goo Dolls. The story goes that the new moniker was inspired by a toy that was featured in a magazine ad—a Goo Goo Doll. It's like they went from a name that sounded like a bad horror movie to something that could grace the shelves of a toy store. Talk about a glow-up! So here we are, with the Goo Goo Dolls, reminding us that sometimes, a name change is all it takes to go from punk to pop.

Green Day

You know, it's funny how names can shape our perceptions, especially in the world of music. Take Green Day, for example. When you hear that name, you might picture a band of rebellious rockers, perhaps strumming their guitars in a haze of youthful angst. But let me take you back to the beginning, where they were known as Sweet Children. Yes, you heard me right—Sweet Children! I mean, can you imagine? Sweet Children sounds more like a group of toddlers singing nursery rhymes than a punk rock band that would eventually take the world by storm.

Picture it: a bunch of scruffy teenagers in California, jamming out with names like "Sweet Children" while their friends are probably rolling their eyes and asking if they're going to perform at a birthday party next. I can just see them in their early gigs, wearing oversized T-shirts and jeans, trying to convince the crowd that they were, in fact, the coolest kids on the block, despite their name sounding like a floral arrangement.

But here's the kicker—Sweet Children was actually a nod to their youthful innocence and the carefree days of adolescence. It's almost poetic, right? But let's be real. When you think about it, there's nothing edgy about a name that sounds like a daycare center. So, they decided to switch things up. Enter Green Day. Now that's a name that screams "We're here to rock your socks off!" It's catchy, it's memorable, and it's got that rebellious flair. Plus, it's a cheeky reference to their love for... well, let's just say, "herbal refreshments."

So, next time you crank up "Boulevard of Broken Dreams," just remember that it all started with a name that might have had you picturing a kindergarten class instead of a rock phenomenon. Sweet Children? Nah, let's stick with Green Day!

No Doubt

Ah, No Doubt, the iconic band that defined a generation with their catchy tunes and Gwen Stefani's unforgettable style. But did you know that before they became the chart-topping sensation we know and love, they had a rather peculiar original name? That's right! They were initially called "Gwen Stefani and the Harajuku Girls," which sounds more like a quirky fashion line than a rock band! Just imagine it: a bunch of punk rockers strutting around in vibrant, Japanese-inspired outfits, while Gwen led the charge with her signature red lips and platinum blonde hair. It's a name that would make anyone think, "Are they here to rock my world or sell me a pair of neon leg warmers?"

But let's dig a little deeper. The name was short-lived, and honestly, it didn't take long for the band to realize that they needed something that screamed "we're here to stay" rather than "we're a one-hit wonder at a cosplay convention." Enter the name "No Doubt." Now, that's a name with some punch! It exudes confidence, like they were saying, "We're so good, you don't even need to question it."

It's a brilliant rebranding move, but can you imagine if they had stuck with the original name? We'd be singing along to "Just a Girl" while surrounded by a sea of Harajuku fashionistas, and the band would probably have a side gig designing accessories!

In hindsight, "No Doubt" was the perfect fit. It allowed them to evolve from a quirky concept into a powerhouse of a band. So, next time you belt out "Don't Speak," just remember: it could have been

"Gwen Stefani and the Harajuku Girls," and we'd all be scratching our heads, wondering where the rock went!

Faith No More

You know, it's funny how names can shape perceptions, especially in the music world. Take, for instance, the iconic band Faith No More. You hear that name, and you think, "Wow, these guys must be deep, maybe a little philosophical." But hold onto your hats because they originally went by a name that sounds like a rejected title for a children's book: "Faith No Man." Yes, you heard that right! Can you imagine walking into a bar and seeing a flyer that says, "Come see Faith No Man!" You'd probably think it was some sort of bizarre anti-masculinity seminar rather than a rock concert.

Now, let's break this down. "Faith No Man" had a certain flair, but it also had a slightly confusing vibe. I mean, what were they trying to say? That faith is exclusive to women? That men are inherently untrustworthy? Or maybe it was just a clever way of saying, "Hey, don't put your faith in us, because we might just rock your socks off and leave you questioning everything!"

But then, the band decided to change their name, and thank goodness for that. "Faith No More" rolls off the tongue like a smooth jazz riff, while "Faith No Man" sounds like a bad sitcom waiting to happen. Imagine the theme song: "Faith No Man, but maybe a dog!"

And let's not forget the irony. With a name like "Faith No More," they went on to become one of the most influential bands of their time, proving that faith in music can indeed transcend all boundaries. So here's to the power of a name! Just think, if they had stuck with "Faith No Man," we might have been deprived of classics like "Epic" and "Midlife Crisis." Now that's a crisis worth avoiding!

Iron Maiden

You know, when you think of iconic rock bands, names like Led Zeppelin or The Rolling Stones come to mind, but let's talk about Iron Maiden for a second. Now, you might think that name conjures images of fierce warriors or heavy metal legends, but the truth is, it all started with a rather... unusual inspiration. Picture this: the band was originally going to be called "Gypsy's Kiss." Yes, you heard me right! Gypsy's Kiss! I can just imagine the band members sitting around, trying to look tough while wearing leather jackets, and then someone says, "How about we name ourselves after a romanticized notion of a wandering fortune-teller's peck on the cheek?" Talk about a name that could use a little more edge!

But wait, it gets better. The band's founder, Steve Harris, was inspired by a medieval torture device called the iron maiden. Now, that's more like it! A giant sarcophagus with spikes on the inside, designed to give its unfortunate occupant a very bad day. I mean, when you're trying to sell records, nothing says "buy my album" like a name that sounds like a horror movie prop. "Come for the music, stay for the existential dread!"

So, Gypsy's Kiss was out, and Iron Maiden was in. And honestly, it's a name that has served them well. It's memorable, it's fierce, and it certainly gets your attention. Imagine if they had stuck with Gypsy's Kiss. Would they have sold out stadiums? Probably not. Instead, they've built a legacy that's as sharp as the spikes in that medieval contraption. So here's to Iron Maiden, the band that went from a whimsical kiss to a heavy metal fist!

Lynyrd Skynyrd

You know, it's funny how names can shape our perceptions, especially when it comes to rock bands. Take Lynyrd Skynyrd, for example. You hear that name and you think of Southern rock, wild guitar riffs, and a certain rebellious spirit. But did you know that the band originally went by a name that sounds more like a character from a bad sitcom than a legendary rock group? That's right! They started out as "My Backyard." Yes, you heard me correctly—My Backyard. Can you imagine? "Hey, did you catch My Backyard at the bar last night?" It sounds like a neighborhood gathering where everyone brings their own potato salad and the biggest drama is who forgot to bring the napkins.

The story goes that the band was formed in the late 1960s, and they were just a bunch of kids jamming in a garage—classic rock and roll origin story, right? But with a name like My Backyard, they might as well have been performing at a family reunion. I can picture it now: "Ladies and gentlemen, put your hands together for My Backyard, playing the hits of the summer!"

Eventually, they changed their name to honor their high school gym teacher, Leonard Skinner, who was notorious for enforcing strict rules about long hair. So, they tweaked it a bit—Lynyrd Skynyrd. It's clever, it's catchy, and it definitely has more edge than My Backyard. I mean, can you imagine "Sweet Home Alabama" being belted out by a band called My Backyard? It just doesn't have the same ring to it. So, here's to Lynyrd Skynyrd—the band that went from backyard barbecues to rock and roll legends, and a name that still makes you want to crank up the volume and drive with the windows down.

The Allman Brothers Band

You know, when you think of iconic rock bands, names like The Rolling Stones or The Beatles come to mind, but let's take a moment to appreciate the original name of the band that would become The Allman Brothers Band. Picture this: it's the late 1960s, a time when flower power was in full bloom, and music was all about peace, love, and... well, some really weird band names. The Allman Brothers were originally going to be called "The Allman Joys." Yes, you heard that right. The Allman Joys. I mean, it sounds like a group of cheerful clowns juggling guitars at a children's party. "Hey kids, welcome to the party! Here's the Allman Joys to entertain you with their hit song, 'Clowning Around in C Major!'"

But let's be real. The name "The Allman Joys" doesn't exactly scream rock 'n' roll. Can you imagine them headlining at Woodstock under that banner? "Ladies and gentlemen, let's give it up for The Allman Joys!" I can see the crowd now, confused, wondering if they should be dancing or looking for cotton candy. It's like naming a metal band "The Heavy Metal Kittens." Cute, but not exactly intimidating.

The band's decision to switch to The Allman Brothers Band was a stroke of genius. It had a certain gravitas, a familial bond that hinted at the deep-rooted Southern rock sound they would become famous for. Plus, it didn't sound like a circus act. The Allman Brothers Band just rolls off the tongue, doesn't it? It's like the name itself is saying, "We're here to rock your socks off, not juggle them." So, here's to the Allman Brothers, who thankfully avoided the fate of being the most cheerful band in rock history!

Alice In Chains

You know, it's funny how names can shape our perceptions, especially in the world of music. Take the legendary grunge band Alice In Chains, for example. Most people think of them as the harbingers of dark, brooding melodies and haunting lyrics, but did you know they originally went by the name "Alice N' Chains"? Yes, you heard that right! Picture a bunch of scruffy young musicians in the early '90s, probably jamming in a garage, trying to come up with a name that screams "we're edgy and we've got angst," and they settle on that. It sounds like a bad pun that would make your grandma chuckle while she sips her tea. "Alice N' Chains" – it's like they were trying to combine the whimsical charm of a children's story with the heavy weight of existential dread.

But wait, it gets better! The name change was driven by a desire to sound more serious, more mysterious, and maybe a little less like a quirky puppet show. They dropped the "N'" and became Alice In Chains, which instantly conjured images of gothic themes and tortured souls. I mean, who wouldn't want to listen to a band with a name that sounds like it could be the title of a horror movie?

And let's not forget the irony here. While they were trying to shed that playful vibe, their music was anything but light-hearted. With lyrics that explored addiction, pain, and loss, Alice In Chains became synonymous with the grunge movement. So, in a way, they went from a name that could have been a punchline to one that resonates with a generation. Who knew a simple tweak could lead to such a monumental shift? If only they had thought of "Chainsaw Alice" instead – now that would have been memorable!

Pink Floyd

You know, it's funny how names can stick with you, like gum on a shoe, or that one friend who insists on calling you by your high school nickname, even though you've long since graduated to adulthood. Take Pink Floyd, for instance. You might think it's a name that just rolls off the tongue, conjuring images of psychedelic colors, spacey sounds, and existential angst. But let me take you back to the band's origins, where the name was a little less... let's say, iconic.

Originally, the band was formed under the name "The Tea Set." Yes, you heard that right. The Tea Set! Can you imagine? A bunch of long-haired rockers strutting around on stage with a name like that? It's like they were preparing for a genteel afternoon gathering instead of a mind-bending rock performance. "Hey, everyone! Welcome to the Tea Set concert! Please, take a seat, and don't forget to pass the scones!"

But here's where it gets interesting. They had to change their name because, surprise, another band was also called The Tea Set. So, in a moment of sheer brilliance—or perhaps desperation—they decided to combine the names of two blues musicians, Pink Anderson and Floyd Council. And just like that, Pink Floyd was born. Who knew that a couple of blues legends would inadvertently give rise to one of the most influential bands in rock history?

So, the next time you listen to "Comfortably Numb" or "Wish You Were Here," just remember: it all started with a name that sounds more suited for a cozy café than a legendary rock band. And hey, if they ever wanted to do a side project, "The Tea Set" could still be a hit—just imagine the merch! Tea bags with the band's logo, anyone?

Boston

You know, when you think of iconic rock bands, Boston is right up there, right? Their sound is unmistakable, their hits are legendary, but did you know that before they were Boston, they had a completely different name? It's true! They were originally called "The Freehold." Now, I don't know about you, but that sounds like a name for a quaint little bed-and-breakfast or a retirement community where everyone sits around knitting sweaters for their cats. "Welcome to The Freehold, where our residents enjoy bingo nights and the occasional shuffleboard tournament."

Imagine trying to sell that band to a record label. "Hey, we're The Freehold! We've got this killer sound, and we're really into... well, freeholding?" I can picture the confused executives scratching their heads, wondering if they should be investing in music or real estate. "What's your vibe? Are you more of a 'let's rock out' or 'let's discuss property taxes' kind of band?"

But then, they made the brilliant decision to change their name to Boston. Ah, now that's catchy! It's straightforward, it's bold, and it immediately evokes images of the city's rich history, the Freedom Trail, and, of course, clam chowder. Who wouldn't want to be associated with that? It's like they went from being the awkward kid in gym class to the prom king overnight.

So, let's raise a glass to the genius who said, "Hey, let's ditch The Freehold and embrace the spirit of Boston!" Because nothing says rock 'n' roll like a name that makes you think of baked beans and Fenway Park. And who knows? Maybe if they had stuck with The Freehold, we'd all be singing "More Than a Feeling" while sipping herbal tea in a cozy armchair instead.

Kansas

You know, it's funny how names can shape our perceptions, especially when it comes to rock bands. Take Kansas, for instance. The band that gave us "Carry On Wayward Son" and "Dust in the Wind." But did you know they almost had a completely different name? Yes, before they were strumming away with their progressive rock anthems, they were known as "Saratoga." Now, let's pause for a moment and think about that. Saratoga! It sounds more like a horse racing track than a band that would eventually rock stadiums. I can just imagine it: "Ladies and gentlemen, welcome to the Saratoga concert, where the only thing racing is your heart when you hear those killer guitar riffs!"

I mean, who would take a band named after a New York town seriously? You can almost hear the confused fans asking, "Are we here to see a band or a horse?" And while we're at it, can you picture the t-shirts? "I saw Saratoga in concert!" Sure, you might get a few puzzled looks, like you just admitted to being a fan of a local knitting club instead of a legendary rock band.

Fortunately, they realized that Saratoga lacked the punch they needed. Kansas, on the other hand, conjures up images of wide-open skies, rolling fields, and a certain Midwestern grit. It's a name that demands attention! So, they made the switch, and the rest is history. The moral of the story? Sometimes you just have to steer clear of names that sound like they belong on a racetrack and embrace something that resonates with the soul. And thank goodness they did, because who knows? We might have been stuck singing, "Dust in the Horse Race." Now that's a catchy tune!

Pure Prairie League

You know, there's a little nugget of rock history that always cracks me up, and it's about the band Pure Prairie League. Now, before they became the beloved country rock ensemble we know today, they had a name that was, let's say, a bit more... shall we say, avant-garde? They originally called themselves "The Purity League." Sounds like a group of overly enthusiastic health nuts, right? I can just picture them standing around at a farmers' market, handing out kale smoothies and lecturing you on the benefits of quinoa. "Hey, you want to join our Purity League? We're all about clean living and avoiding gluten like it's the plague!"

But wait, it gets better. They quickly realized that "The Purity League" sounded less like a rock band and more like a cult that meets every Tuesday to discuss the merits of organic tofu. So, they decided to shake things up a bit. They thought, "Let's add some prairie flair!" and thus, "Pure Prairie League" was born. Suddenly, they went from being the poster children for a health food store to a band that could belt out tunes about love lost and whiskey found under the wide-open sky.

You have to admire their creativity. I mean, who wouldn't want to be part of a league that sounds like it promotes both purity and a good time? The name change was like taking off a pair of sensible shoes and putting on some cowboy boots. It was a transformation from a group that might have been handing out pamphlets on the dangers of sugar to one that's jamming out at a honky-tonk bar, singing about heartbreak, freedom, and maybe a little too much bourbon. So here's to Pure Prairie League, a name that truly captures the spirit of rock and roll—pure, prairie, and unapologetically fun!

Oasis

You know, it's funny how names can shape our perceptions. Take the rock band Oasis, for instance. When you hear "Oasis," you probably think of sun-soaked beaches, refreshing drinks, and maybe a little bit of that '90s Britpop magic. But here's the kicker: they almost didn't go with that name at all. Originally, they were called "The Rain." Yes, "The Rain." Can you imagine? Instead of catchy anthems like "Wonderwall," we'd be singing along to "Here Comes the Rain Again." It's a bit like naming a dog "Fido" and then realizing he's more of a "Bark Twain."

The story goes that Noel Gallagher, the band's creative genius, was not exactly thrilled with the name. I mean, who could blame him? "The Rain" sounds like a group of moody teenagers huddled under an umbrella, strumming their guitars while contemplating life's deepest questions. It's not exactly the vibe you want when you're trying to conquer the world of rock and roll.

So, how did they land on "Oasis"? Well, it turns out they were inspired by a local music venue called Oasis Leisure Centre. Imagine the band sitting around, pondering their identity, and someone pipes up with, "Hey, let's name ourselves after that place where we used to play dodgeball." Genius! They went from being a gloomy weather forecast to a refreshing retreat. Who wouldn't want to be associated with a lush, green escape?

In the end, "Oasis" captured the essence of their sound—uplifting, vibrant, and a bit of a getaway from the dreariness of everyday life. So, here's to the name change that brought us some of the most iconic tunes of the '90s. I guess sometimes, you just need a little sunshine to brighten your day!

Blood, Sweat, and Tears

You know, when you think of iconic bands, names like The Rolling Stones or The Beatles come to mind, right? But let's take a moment to talk about Blood, Sweat and Tears. Sounds intense, doesn't it? It conjures images of epic battles and heroic sacrifices, maybe even a few tears shed over a broken heart. But believe it or not, the original name of this legendary band was... wait for it... "The Electric Flag." Yes, you heard that right! The Electric Flag! Sounds like a superhero team that fights crime with the power of rock, doesn't it?

Imagine a group of musicians dressed in spandex, capes flapping in the wind, strumming electric guitars while battling the forces of mediocrity. But here's the kicker: The Electric Flag was already taken by another band! Talk about bad luck! It's like trying to name your new pet "Fluffy" only to discover that your neighbor has a cat by the same name.

So, what do you do when life hands you lemons? You squeeze them into a catchy name that sounds like a gritty 70s action movie. Blood, Sweat and Tears! It's a name that screams, "We're serious about our music, and we're not afraid to get a little messy!" I mean, who wouldn't want to listen to a band that sounds like they've just run a marathon, climbed a mountain, and had a good cry all in one sitting?

And let's be honest, it's a name that sticks with you. You might forget who sang that catchy tune from the '70s, but you'll never forget Blood, Sweat and Tears. It's a name that's as unforgettable as the music itself, and honestly, it's probably the most accurate description of what it takes to make it in the music industry!

Porno For Pyros

You know, I've always been fascinated by band names. They can be a reflection of a band's identity, their sound, or sometimes, just a random collection of words that somehow seem to fit. Take Porno For Pyros, for instance. Now, that's a name that raises eyebrows and perhaps a few chuckles. But did you know that their original name was actually "The Pigs"? Yes, you heard that right—The Pigs! It's almost as if they were trying to channel their inner farm animal, which, let's be honest, doesn't quite scream rock 'n' roll.

Imagine the band's first gig: "Ladies and gentlemen, please welcome to the stage... The Pigs!" I can just picture the confused looks on people's faces. "Wait, are we at a concert or a barbecue?" The name had potential, sure, but it lacked that spark, that edge that makes you want to jump out of your seat and scream. So, they decided to switch it up. And thank goodness they did! "Porno For Pyros" is a name that grabs you by the collar and demands your attention. It's audacious, it's provocative, and it's definitely not something you'd forget in a hurry.

Now, you might wonder about the meaning behind it. Was it a commentary on society? A nod to the absurdity of modern life? Or maybe just a way to get people to stop and think, "What on earth does that even mean?" The beauty of it is that it doesn't need to mean anything profound. It's just a catchy phrase that makes you giggle, raises an eyebrow, and gets you curious about the music. So here's to the evolution of band names, and to the glorious moment when The Pigs became Porno For Pyros! Rock on, my friends, rock on!

Jane's Addiction

You know, there's a fascinating little tidbit about the legendary band Jane's Addiction that most people probably don't know, and it's a story that's as colorful as the band's music itself. Before they became the iconic alternative rock group we know today, they were originally called... wait for it... "Jane's Addiction to Pornography." Yes, you heard that right! Can you imagine the poor radio DJs trying to announce that? "And now, here's Jane's Addiction to Pornography with their latest hit!" I mean, talk about a mouthful!

The name was a reflection of the band's wild, hedonistic lifestyle in Los Angeles during the late '80s, a time when excess was practically a cultural requirement. But let's be honest, who wouldn't want to rock out to a band with a name like that? It screams "party" louder than a frat house on a Saturday night. But, as with all good things, there comes a time for a rebranding. The band realized that maybe, just maybe, they should tone it down a notch. So, they dropped the "to Pornography" part, and just like that, they became Jane's Addiction. It's like going from "party animal" to "party enthusiast"—still fun, but a little less likely to get you kicked out of your parents' house.

But think about it: the original name was a perfect encapsulation of the band's ethos, their raw energy, and the chaotic world they were living in. They were all about pushing boundaries, and what better way to do that than with a name that could make your grandma clutch her pearls? So, here's to Jane's Addiction, the band that knew how to rock hard while keeping it just PG enough for the mainstream. Rock on, and remember, it's all in the name!

Red Hot Chili Peppers

You know, it's funny how names can shape our perceptions. Take the rock band Red Hot Chili Peppers, for instance. When you hear that name, you might picture a fiery, spicy explosion of sound, right? But did you know that their original name was—drumroll, please—Tony Flow and the Miraculously Majestic Masters of Mayhem? Yes, you heard that right! It sounds like a circus act, doesn't it? I can just imagine them rolling into town, setting up a tent, and offering cotton candy along with a side of funky bass lines.

Now, when you think of a band that would give you a wild ride through funk and rock, you probably don't envision a bunch of guys named Tony Flow. I mean, "Tony Flow"? It sounds like the name of a guy who'd be more comfortable at a deli than on stage. "Hey, Tony Flow, can you pass me the mustard?" But here's the kicker: this name was a reflection of their early sound, which was more chaotic and experimental than the polished grooves we know today. It was like a musical buffet where you weren't sure if you were going to get a spicy salsa or just a big ol' plate of confusion.

Eventually, they realized that "Tony Flow" just wasn't going to cut it if they wanted to be taken seriously. So, they switched to Red Hot Chili Peppers, a name that conjures up images of a vibrant, energetic band that can make you dance like nobody's watching. It's catchy, it's memorable, and it doesn't make you feel like you need to ask for a refund on your ticket. So, next time you rock out to their hits, just remember: it all started with Tony Flow, the king of mayhem, who probably never imagined he'd be overshadowed by a spicy vegetable!

They Might Be Giants

You know, it's funny how names can shape our perceptions. Take the band They Might Be Giants, for instance. You hear that name and you think, "Wow, these guys must be some sort of whimsical giants, perhaps lumbering through the land, spreading joy and catchy tunes!" But let me take you back to their original name, which was… drumroll, please… The They Might Be Giants Band! Yes, truly, that was the extent of their creativity at the time. I mean, it's like calling a dog "Doggy the Dog." Not exactly a groundbreaking choice, right?

Now, picture this: a group of quirky musicians in the early '80s, huddled in a basement, trying to come up with a name that screams "we're unique!" and they land on something that sounds like a half-hearted attempt at a school project. "Hey, what do you think of 'The They Might Be Giants Band'?" It's like they were trying to be the most polite rock band in history. "We might be giants, but we're definitely not imposing! Please, call us by our full name!"

But here's where it gets interesting. The name was inspired by the 1971 film "They Might Be Giants," starring George C. Scott, who believes he's Sherlock Holmes. So, you've got this band channeling the spirit of a man who thinks he's a detective while simultaneously sounding like a bunch of overzealous college students trying to impress their professor.

Eventually, they trimmed it down to They Might Be Giants, which has a nice ring to it. It's mysterious, it's playful, and it gives off just the right amount of "we're not taking ourselves too seriously." And that, my friends, is how a band went from a mouthful to a name that's now synonymous with quirky brilliance. Who knew a name could have such a journey?

Blind Melon

You know, it's funny how names can shape perceptions, right? Take the band Blind Melon, for instance. You might think that name conjures up images of hippie vibes and flower power, but let me take you back to the late '80s when they were originally called—drumroll, please—"The Buds." Yes, you heard me right. The Buds! I can just imagine them on stage, surrounded by bright lights, playing their hearts out, and the audience chanting, "Go Buds!" It sounds like a high school pep rally, not a rock concert.

Now, I get it. "The Buds" has that laid-back, friendly vibe, like a group of guys you'd invite over for a barbecue. But let's be honest, it's not exactly the name that screams, "We're here to change the world with our music!" It's more like, "We're here to change the world with our potato salad recipe."

So, how did they land on "Blind Melon"? Well, legend has it that the name came from a combination of a blind melon and a whimsical thought process. Apparently, one of the band members had this vision of a blind melon rolling down a hill. And if you think about it, it's kind of poetic. A blind melon—completely unaware of its surroundings, just rolling along, living its best life. It's a metaphor for the carefree spirit of the '90s!

But let's be real, "Blind Melon" is just a cooler name. It has that edge, that mystery. It begs questions. Like, what does a blind melon even look like? Is it sad? Happy? Does it know it's blind? So, here's to Blind Melon, the band that went from the Buds to a name that's as memorable as their catchy tunes. Who knew a fruit could be so profound?

Hootie and the Blowfish

You know, when you think of iconic '90s bands, Hootie and the Blowfish immediately comes to mind—right up there with grunge and questionable fashion choices. But did you ever stop and wonder about their original name? Spoiler alert: it wasn't always Hootie and the Blowfish. In fact, the band started out as "The Wolf Brothers." Yes, you heard that right! Picture it: a bunch of college kids in South Carolina, jamming out in their dorm rooms, calling themselves The Wolf Brothers. It sounds like a bad reality show about siblings who can't stop arguing over who gets the last slice of pizza.

Now, you might think, "What's wrong with that?" Well, let me tell you, "The Wolf Brothers" sounds like a band that would be playing at your cousin's wedding—complete with a questionable cover of "Sweet Caroline" and a lot of awkward shuffling on the dance floor. So, they decided to change things up. Enter Hootie. Legend has it that Hootie was actually a nickname for one of their friends, a guy who had a big head and an even bigger heart. And "The Blowfish"? Well, that's a mystery wrapped in an enigma, but it's definitely fun to imagine a fish that blows up when it gets scared—just like the band's music did when they hit the charts!

So, there you have it. From The Wolf Brothers to Hootie and the Blowfish, they transformed into a household name. Who knew that a big-headed friend and a fish that inflates could lead to one of the most memorable names in music history? And honestly, if they hadn't made that change, we'd all be reminiscing about The Wolf Brothers' "Tales from the Dorm Room" instead of belting out "I Only Want to Be With You" at karaoke night.

Maroon 5

You know, it's funny how names can shape perceptions, right? Take Maroon 5, for instance. We all know them for their catchy tunes and Adam Levine's unmistakable voice, but did you know they didn't start off as Maroon 5? Oh no, my friends. They were once known as Kara's Flowers. Yes, Kara's Flowers! It sounds like a local florist or a high school band that played at prom. Imagine that!

Picture it: a bunch of teenage boys, probably still figuring out their hair gel, strumming away at their guitars, dreaming of rock stardom while the name "Kara's Flowers" rolls off their tongues like a bad pun. I mean, who was Kara? Was she the girl they all had crushes on? Did she break one of their hearts? Did she have a pet rock named Flower? The possibilities are endless, but let's be honest, it's hard to rock out to "Kara's Flowers" without picturing floral arrangements and pastel colors.

Fast forward to their transition to Maroon 5, and suddenly they're a global sensation. They went from prom band to pop icons, all because they ditched the floral theme for something a little more... well, maroon. It's a color, it's a mood, it's a band name that actually sounds like it belongs on the charts instead of a school talent show.

And can we talk about the color maroon? It's like red's cooler, more sophisticated cousin who went to art school and drinks espresso instead of soda. So, here's to Maroon 5, the band that blossomed from a floral fiasco into a powerhouse of pop. Who knew a name change could be the secret ingredient to success? Now, if only they could have changed their name to something even cooler, like "Rock 'n' Roll Unicorns." Now that would have been a sight to see!

The Bangles

You know, it's funny how names can shape a band's identity, right? Take The Bangles, for example. Before they became the pop-rock darlings of the '80s, they were known as The Bangs. Yes, The Bangs! I mean, talk about a name that screams "we're here to rock your socks off" while simultaneously making you think of a bad haircut from the '90s. Imagine the confusion! You're at a concert, and you're like, "Hey, did you catch The Bangs last night?" and your friend is like, "You mean the haircut or the band?"

The name change came about because, believe it or not, there was another band already using the name The Bangs. I can picture the moment they found out. They're huddled in a garage, practicing their harmonies, and someone bursts in with the news: "Guys, we can't be The Bangs anymore! There's a band in New Jersey that's already claiming that title!" Cue the collective groan. What do you do? You brainstorm, of course!

So, they decided to take a cue from their love of fashion and jewelry, and thus, The Bangles were born. Now, they're not just a band; they're a whole vibe! And let's be real, "The Bangles" has a much more glamorous ring to it. It conjures images of colorful bracelets jangling as they perform "Walk Like an Egyptian." It's catchy, it's memorable, and it definitely beats the idea of being forever associated with a bad hair day.

So, the next time you hear "Eternal Flame" or "Manic Monday," just remember: it could have been a lot worse. They could have been rocking out as The Bangs, and we'd all be stuck with hair product jokes instead of catchy tunes!

The Go-Gos

So, let's take a stroll down memory lane, shall we? Picture it: Los Angeles, 1978, a time when bell-bottoms were still a thing, and disco balls ruled the dance floors. Enter a group of fierce women who were about to shake up the music scene. But before they became the iconic Go-Go's, they were known by a name that, well, let's just say it lacked a certain... pizzazz. They called themselves The Misfits. Yes, The Misfits! I mean, can you imagine that? The Misfits? It sounds more like a group of kids who just can't find their way home after a school field trip rather than the trailblazing band that would give us "We Got the Beat."

The story goes that the name was inspired by their rebellious spirit, but let's be honest, it also sounded like a bad sitcom about a family of lovable outcasts. Picture it: the Misfits living in a quirky house, getting into zany adventures while trying to navigate the music industry. They'd probably have a pet parrot named "Harmony" who squawks out catchy hooks.

But here's the kicker: the name was already taken by a punk band from New Jersey. Talk about a buzzkill! So, the girls, ever resourceful, decided to change their name. They wanted something that screamed fun, energy, and girl power—something that would make you want to dance. Enter The Go-Go's, a name that evokes images of high-energy dance parties and neon leg warmers.

And just like that, The Misfits faded into obscurity, while The Go-Go's became legends, proving that sometimes a name can make all the difference. So, next time you hear "Our Lips Are Sealed," just remember: it could have been "The Misfits," and we'd all be dancing to a sitcom theme song instead!

DEVO

You know, it's funny how names can shape our perception of things. Take the band DEVO, for example. When you hear "DEVO," you probably think of that quirky, new wave group with their iconic energy dome hats and a sound that's a delightful mix of synth and punk. But did you know that before they became DEVO, they were known as something that sounds like a rejected name for a 90s tech startup? That's right! They were originally called "De-Evolution." Yeah, you heard me! De-Evolution! It's like they were trying to warn us that society was regressing, one synth riff at a time.

Imagine walking into a bar and saying, "Hey, have you heard the latest from De-Evolution?" It sounds like they'd be playing a set of songs about the decline of civilization while simultaneously serving you a cocktail named "The Social Deterioration." Not exactly the vibe you want for a night out, right?

But here's the kicker: the concept of de-evolution was serious business for them. They believed that society was regressing rather than progressing, which is a pretty heavy thought. But they packaged it in such a way that you could dance to it! They took their angst and wrapped it in catchy tunes and bizarre costumes.

So, in a way, changing their name to DEVO was genius. It's snappy, it's catchy, and it's a lot easier to yell at a concert. "DEVO!" just rolls off the tongue, while "De-Evolution!" sounds like a lecture you'd rather skip. So next time you hear "Whip It," remember that behind those catchy beats is a band that once thought we were all heading straight for the Stone Age—while still managing to throw a killer dance party!

The Grateful Dead

You know, when you think of rock legends, names like The Rolling Stones or Led Zeppelin pop into your head, but have you ever pondered the origins of the name "The Grateful Dead"? It's a name that conjures up images of tie-dye shirts, swirling psychedelic colors, and a certain, shall we say, "expanded state of consciousness." But believe it or not, they weren't always the Grateful Dead. Nope! They started off as "The Warlocks." Now, doesn't that sound like a band that would be opening for a Dungeons & Dragons convention? "Ladies and gentlemen, welcome to the stage, The Warlocks! Prepare for an evening of enchanted riffs and magical solos!"

So, how did they go from Warlocks to Grateful Dead? Well, legend has it that the band discovered another group had already claimed the name Warlocks. I mean, can you imagine the disappointment? "Hey, guys, we can't be The Warlocks anymore." "What? But I just bought a wizard hat!" So, they needed a new name, and that's when the cosmos intervened.

They stumbled upon a book of folklore, and there it was: "The Grateful Dead." It's actually a term that refers to a story where a dead person is helped by someone they've helped in life. It's a beautiful concept, but let's be real—when you hear that name, you think of a band that's probably been to the other side and back. I mean, how many bands can say their name is inspired by a dead guy getting a helping hand?

So, next time you're jamming to "Touch of Grey," just remember: they could've been Warlocks. And honestly, I'm not sure if that would've been more or less cool. Either way, we're all just grateful they didn't settle for "The Warlocks."

The Pretenders

You know, there's something oddly delightful about the history of rock bands, especially when you dive into their original names. Take The Pretenders, for example. Now, when you hear that name, you might think of some cool, edgy group that's all about rebellion and attitude. But let me take you back to the late '70s, when they were just a bunch of musicians trying to find their footing in the chaotic world of rock and roll. Their original name? The Swinging Cats. Yes, you heard that right. The Swinging Cats! I mean, can you imagine that? A name that conjures up images of jazz clubs, feline dance-offs, and maybe a catnip-fueled jam session.

Picture it: a smoky bar, a crowd of leather-clad rockers, and then, out comes The Swinging Cats, ready to unleash their sound. I can just see the bewildered faces in the audience, thinking, "Are we here for a concert or a cat show?" It's hard to take a band seriously when you're picturing them in tuxedos, bow ties, and maybe even a little top hat, swaying to the rhythm of a catnip-infused ballad.

Of course, they eventually realized that The Swinging Cats wasn't quite the image they wanted to project. So, they decided to go with The Pretenders, which, let's be honest, has a much cooler vibe. It's mysterious, it's rebellious, and it sounds like they might just be pretending to be something they're not—like a cat pretending to be a lion.

So, the next time you hear "Brass in Pocket," just remember that somewhere in the annals of rock history, there's a band that almost made it big as The Swinging Cats, and that's a legacy worth a chuckle.

Blondie

So, let's talk about Blondie, the iconic band that brought us catchy tunes and a whole lot of style. But did you know they almost went by a completely different name? Picture this: it's the early 1970s in New York City, a time when the streets were alive with punk and new wave, and a group of misfits was trying to make their mark. The original name of the band was, wait for it, "The Stilettoes." Yes, you heard that right! The Stilettoes! I mean, it sounds like a name for a shoe store or a trendy nail salon, not a rock band that would later give us classics like "Heart of Glass" and "Call Me."

Can you imagine the confusion? "Hey, did you hear The Stilettoes are playing at CBGB this weekend?" People would show up expecting a fashion show rather than a high-energy performance. And let's be real, how many tough guys in leather jackets would want to tell their friends they were going to see a band called The Stilettoes? It's hard to strike fear into the hearts of your enemies when your band's name sounds like it belongs on a pair of heels!

But then, in a stroke of genius—or perhaps desperation—the band's frontwoman, Debbie Harry, suggested they change it to Blondie, inspired by the nickname she received from a truck driver who couldn't get over her platinum locks. Suddenly, they transformed from a group that sounded like they might be serving cocktails at a bar to a powerhouse band that would dominate the charts. Blondie was born, and the rest is history! So, next time you're dancing to "One Way or Another," just remember, it could have been a lot more fabulous if they were still The Stilettoes!

The Police

You know, it's fascinating how some of the biggest names in music start out with names that are, well, less than iconic. Take The Police, for example. When you think of them, you might picture Sting's sultry voice and those catchy bass lines, but did you know they almost went by a name that sounds like a bad sitcom? That's right! They were originally called "The Strontium 90." Now, if that doesn't sound like a band that plays in your high school gym on a Friday night, I don't know what does.

Strontium 90! It's like they took the most boring element from the periodic table and decided to make it their brand. I mean, what were they thinking? "Hey guys, let's name ourselves after a radioactive isotope! That'll really get the crowds going!" Can you imagine the band's merch? "Get your Strontium 90 t-shirts! Wear it to your next science fair!"

But, to be fair, they did have a point. Strontium 90 is linked to nuclear fallout, and what better way to describe their explosive sound? Yet, I can just picture the confused looks on fans' faces. "Hey, do you want to go see Strontium 90 tonight?" "Uh, do they play rock or do they just talk about nuclear chemistry?"

Eventually, they realized that a name like The Police would have a much better ring to it. It's catchy, it's memorable, and it evokes a certain authority—like they're here to enforce the law of rock 'n' roll. So next time you hear "Roxanne," just remember, it could have been a lot weirder. Instead of "Roxanne," we could've been singing, "Hey, Strontium 90, don't you be so mean!" Now that's a song I'd like to hear!

Chicago

You know, most people think of Chicago as the Windy City, a hub of deep-dish pizza, and a place where the blues were born. But did you know it was almost known for something much more absurd? Originally, the rock band Chicago, that iconic group that gave us hits like "25 or 6 to 4," was actually called "The Big Thing." Yes, you heard that right—The Big Thing. Can you imagine if they had stuck with that name? "Hey, have you heard The Big Thing's new album?" It just sounds like a strange conversation about a new diet fad or a particularly large piece of furniture.

The Big Thing had a certain charm, sure, but it lacked the punch that "Chicago" delivers. I mean, Chicago is a city with grit, history, and a serious jazz scene. The Big Thing? That sounds like a local diner's special on a Tuesday. "Come on down for The Big Thing! It's a mystery meat surprise!"

The name change happened in 1969, and thank goodness for that. I can't picture the band performing at the Super Bowl with a name like The Big Thing. "And now, please welcome The Big Thing!" Cue the crickets.

What's even funnier is that they were initially worried about the name Chicago being too "geographic." As if people wouldn't want to listen to a band named after a city! I mean, look at New York, Los Angeles, even Boston! All these cities have bands named after them. But Chicago? That's a name that resonates. It's got character!

So here's to the band that almost was The Big Thing. They've come a long way, and thankfully, they're not just a quirky trivia question anymore. They're a rock legend, and that's no small thing!

Toto

You know, it's funny how names can shape perceptions, right? Like, take the rock band Toto, for instance. When you hear "Toto," what do you think of? A cute little dog from Oz? A catchy pop tune? Well, here's the kicker: the original name of the band was actually "The Blessed Event." I mean, really? The Blessed Event? It sounds like a church potluck or a baby shower, not a rock band that would go on to give us "Africa" and "Hold the Line." Can you imagine the band introducing themselves on stage? "Ladies and gentlemen, please welcome The Blessed Event!" I can just picture the confused looks on the audience's faces, half expecting a sermon instead of a guitar solo.

But let's be real; the name change was probably a stroke of genius. "Toto" is short, snappy, and rolls off the tongue like a well-placed drumbeat. It's also memorable. I mean, who wouldn't remember a band named after a dog? It's like they took a cue from the Wizard of Oz and decided to embrace their inner pop culture. And let's not forget, the band members were all seasoned musicians—session players, in fact—so they probably knew that a name like "The Blessed Event" wasn't going to get them any radio play.

It's almost like they were saying, "Hey, we're here to rock, not to bless your baby!" So, they settled on Toto, a name that would carry them through the '70s and '80s, making them legends in their own right. Who knew that a name change could lead to such a fruitful career? So, here's to Toto—the band that proves sometimes, a little rebranding can go a long way. And who knows, maybe they'll turn up at that baby shower after all!

Styx

You know, it's funny how names can shape our perceptions, right? Take the rock band Styx, for instance. You probably think of them as the purveyors of epic rock ballads and cosmic themes, but did you know they almost had a completely different name? That's right! Before they became the iconic band we know today, they were originally called "The Tradewinds." Now, I don't know about you, but when I hear "The Tradewinds," I picture a group of guys in Hawaiian shirts, sipping piña coladas, and strumming ukuleles on a beach somewhere. Not exactly the vibe of a band that would later give us "Come Sail Away," right?

So, what happened? Well, apparently, the name didn't quite capture their musical essence. I mean, who wants to rock out to a band that sounds like they'd be headlining a luau? They needed something that screamed "we're serious about our rock and roll," and "The Tradewinds" just didn't cut it. So, they decided to dig deep into mythology and came up with "Styx," named after the river in Greek mythology that separates the living from the dead. Talk about a name with gravitas!

But let's be real here. Styx sounds cool, but it also sounds like a band that might be performing at a haunted house or a Halloween party, right? "Welcome to the stage, Styx! Prepare for a night of rock and roll... and possibly some ghostly apparitions!"

In the end, they made the right choice. "Styx" has a certain ring to it, a certain mystique, while "The Tradewinds" just sounds like a band that would be playing soft rock at your aunt's wedding. So here's to Styx, the band that defied the tropics and embraced the mythical!

The Little River Band

You know, there's something oddly charming about the way band names evolve. Take the Little River Band, for instance. When you hear that name, you might picture a serene, sun-dappled river, perhaps with a couple of ducks paddling along, or maybe a bunch of musicians sitting around a campfire, strumming their guitars and singing harmoniously about love and life. But let me take you back to the original name of this iconic Australian band: The Zoot. Yes, you heard that right—The Zoot! Now, that's a name that conjures up images of psychedelic colors and bell-bottoms, not exactly the mellow vibe of a little river.

The Zoot was formed in the late 1960s, and they were a band that truly encapsulated the spirit of the times. They were wild, they were loud, and they were definitely not afraid to let their freak flag fly. But as the years rolled on, they realized that maybe, just maybe, they needed a name that resonated a bit more with the adult contemporary crowd. Enter the Little River Band, a name that suggests tranquility and a hint of nostalgia. It's like they went from being the wild party at the end of the street to the cozy gathering at grandma's house, complete with freshly baked cookies and soft rock tunes.

Imagine the conversation: "Hey, guys, we need to rebrand. How about we ditch The Zoot and go for something that sounds more like a relaxing vacation?" And thus, the Little River Band was born. It's a classic case of "let's grow up, but not too much." So, the next time you hear "Reminiscing" playing on the radio, just remember, it all started with a name that was a little too zany for the mellow vibe they eventually embraced.

Asia

You know, it's funny how some of the biggest names in music have origins that are just as bizarre as their hits. Take the band Asia, for example. You might think, "Ah, Asia, the land of rich culture and history." But did you know that the original name of the band was actually "Geography Class"? Yes, you heard me right! Imagine walking into a concert and hearing the lead singer shout, "Welcome to Geography Class! Hope you didn't forget your maps!"

The band was formed by members of other famous groups, and they wanted a name that reflected their global aspirations. But "Geography Class"? It sounds like a group of high school students trying to win a talent show, not a rock band that would go on to sell millions of albums. Can you picture it? Instead of "Heat of the Moment," we'd be jamming to "The Capital Cities of the World."

Eventually, the band decided that "Geography Class" wasn't going to cut it. They needed something with a bit more flair, something that screamed "We're here to rock your socks off!" So, they settled on "Asia." It was catchy, it was sleek, and it had that exotic appeal. Plus, it didn't require a pop quiz to remember.

But let's be honest: if they had stuck with "Geography Class," they might have sparked a whole new genre—academic rock! Picture it: "The Great Lakes Medley" or "The Continents Shuffle." I can see it now, a band of nerds rocking out in plaid shirts, teaching us all about tectonic plates while shredding on electric guitars. So next time you hear "Only Time Will Tell," just remember, it could have been "Only Time Will Tell You Where Mongolia Is."

The Eagles

You know, it's funny how names can shape our perceptions, right? Take the rock band The Eagles, for instance. When you hear "The Eagles," you probably picture soaring melodies, harmonies that could make angels weep, and a laid-back vibe that says, "Yeah, I'm cool with just hanging out." But did you know that before they became the iconic Eagles we know today, they almost went with a name that could have landed them in a completely different genre?

Originally, they toyed with the name "The Pigeons." Yes, you heard that right—The Pigeons! Can you imagine? "Hotel California" would have taken on a whole new meaning. Instead of "You can check out any time you like," it would be more like, "You can flock away anytime you like." And let's face it, pigeons aren't exactly the most glamorous birds. They're more associated with pecking at crumbs in city parks than rocking out in arenas.

Now, I get it; they were probably going for something relatable, something that screamed "everyman." But "The Pigeons" sounds like a band that would play at your local coffee shop, covering Simon & Garfunkel while your barista rolls her eyes. "Oh great, another pigeon song."

Then there's the imagery. Eagles are majestic, powerful, soaring above the clouds, while pigeons... well, they're just kind of there, waddling around, looking for stale bread. Imagine the album covers! Instead of a fierce eagle with wings spread wide, we'd have a cartoonish pigeon with a beanie, maybe a little skateboard under its wing.

So, thank goodness for that last-minute change. The Eagles soared into rock history, and The Pigeons? They're still just hanging out in the park, cooing about their missed opportunity.

Wings

Imagine a world where the legendary band Wings, known for their catchy melodies and Paul McCartney's unmistakable charm, had a completely different name. Yes, folks, before they soared to fame, they were almost called "The Plastic Mac Band." Now, let that sink in for a moment. The Plastic Mac Band! It sounds like an off-brand toy you'd find in a discount bin, right next to the "Action Figures of Historical Figures" collection. Picture kids unwrapping their Christmas gifts, only to find a Paul McCartney action figure made of the same material as a cheap raincoat. Who wouldn't want to rock out with a band that sounds like they were formed in a recycling plant?

The name "Wings" was chosen for its uplifting connotations, evoking images of freedom and flight. But "Plastic Mac"? It conjures up thoughts of something that might melt in the sun. You can almost hear the parents sighing, "Oh great, another band named after a cheap kitchen utensil." I mean, who wants to tell their friends they're going to see Plastic Mac live? You'd have to explain that no, it's not a cooking show, and yes, they do play music—sort of.

It's a wonder they didn't go with "The Beatle Boppers" or "McCartney's Mini-Mes." Thank goodness for that moment of clarity when they decided to embrace the concept of wings. After all, who wouldn't want to fly away from the idea of being tied to a name that sounds like a failed science experiment? In the end, Wings became a symbol of creativity and innovation, while The Plastic Mac Band remains a humorous footnote in the annals of rock history—a reminder that sometimes, the best ideas come with a little bit of ridiculousness.

Gin Blossoms

You know, it's funny how names can shape our perceptions of things. Take, for instance, the rock band Gin Blossoms. When you hear that name, you probably think of something cool, maybe a little rebellious, possibly even a hint of mystery. But did you know that before they were the Gin Blossoms, they went by a name that could only be described as... well, let's say less than rock star-worthy? They were originally called the "Gin Blossoms" after a line in a poem by a guy named Wallace Stevens. Sounds sophisticated, right? But before that, they had a name that could make you cringe just a little: "The Gas Huffer." I mean, wow, talk about a name that could clear a room faster than a bad cologne!

Imagine being at a bar and trying to get people excited about seeing "The Gas Huffer" live. You'd probably get a lot of raised eyebrows and people pretending they had to make an urgent phone call. "Oh, sorry, I can't stay, I just remembered I left my oven on!"

So, they changed their name to something that evoked a bit more charm and whimsy. "Gin Blossoms" sounds like you're about to sip a refreshing cocktail while lounging in a garden, not like you're about to witness a band that might just blow up your speakers.

But here's the kicker: the name change didn't just save them from sounding like a bad high school punk band; it also became a symbol of their music. It encapsulated the bittersweet melodies and lyrics that defined their sound. So, next time you jam out to "Hey Jealousy," remember that behind that catchy tune lies a story of transformation from "Gas Huffer" to "Gin Blossoms." Now that's a glow-up worth celebrating!

Hole

You know, when you think of iconic bands, names like The Beatles, The Rolling Stones, and, of course, Hole come to mind. But did you know that Hole almost had a completely different name? That's right! Before they settled on the name Hole, they toyed with a title that was, shall we say, a bit more... unconventional. Picture this: a band of punk rockers, fiercely rebellious and unapologetic, debating over what to call themselves, and the original suggestion was "The Rumpus Room." I mean, come on! The Rumpus Room? It sounds more like a cozy playroom for toddlers than a grunge band ready to take on the world!

Can you imagine Courtney Love belting out "Rumpus Room" in front of a packed crowd? The audience would be scratching their heads, wondering if they accidentally stumbled into a children's party instead of a rock concert. "Hey, everybody! Welcome to The Rumpus Room! Now, let's get this party started with our hit single, 'Snack Time!'"

But really, let's break down the name. "Rumpus" evokes images of playful chaos, bouncing around like a bunch of hyper kids after too much sugar. It's like they were trying to capture the spirit of rebellion but ended up with a name that belongs on a daycare brochure.

Eventually, they settled on Hole, which is a much more fitting name, if you ask me. It's raw, it's gritty, and it perfectly encapsulates the depths of angst and emotion that the band is known for. So, thank goodness they ditched The Rumpus Room! Can you imagine the t-shirts? "I survived The Rumpus Room tour!" No, thank you! Hole may not have been the original choice, but it certainly became a name that resonates with a generation, and that's no laughing matter—unless you're still stuck in the playroom!

Bachman-Turner Overdrive

Imagine a world where the legendary rock band Bachman Turner Overdrive was known by a completely different name. Yes, folks, before they became the iconic sound of the '70s, they were almost branded as something entirely less cool. Picture this: they were originally called "Brave Belt." Now, I don't know about you, but when I hear "Brave Belt," I think of a superhero accessory or maybe some sort of medieval armor. Can you imagine the album covers? Instead of leather jackets and guitars, we'd have guys in tights and capes, posing with their "brave belts" like they just emerged from a comic book.

Now, let's break this down. The name "Brave Belt" sounds like something you'd find at a thrift store, right next to a pair of bell-bottoms and a lava lamp. It's like they were trying to channel their inner warrior, but all we got was a confused fashion statement. I mean, who wants to be remembered as the band that could have been mistaken for a wrestling tag team? "And now, entering the ring, it's Brave Belt! They're here to rock your socks off... or maybe just mildly entertain you!"

But then, like a phoenix rising from the ashes, they reinvented themselves. Enter Randy Bachman and Fred Turner, and voilà! Bachman Turner Overdrive was born, a name that screamed rock 'n' roll and not a hint of spandex. Suddenly, they were producing hits like "Takin' Care of Business" and "You Ain't Seen Nothing Yet," instead of songs about, I don't know, the virtues of bravery and belt-wearing.

So here's to Bachman Turner Overdrive, the band that went from "Brave Belt" to rock royalty, proving that sometimes, all you need is a name change to unleash your true potential.

Electric Light Orchestra

So, let's take a moment to appreciate the sheer brilliance of the name "Electric Light Orchestra." It rolls off the tongue like a well-rehearsed symphony, doesn't it? But here's the kicker: before they became the iconic band we know today, they were almost called... wait for it... "The Move." Yes, just "The Move." It sounds like a dance instruction or a questionable yoga pose. "Hey, everyone! Let's do The Move!" You can picture it now: a bunch of people awkwardly swaying side to side, wondering if they should be moving their arms or just standing still like confused statues.

Originally, The Move was a rock band that dabbled in pop and psychedelic sounds, but they decided to evolve. They wanted to incorporate orchestral elements into their music, because why not? Who wouldn't want to rock out to a symphony while simultaneously trying to figure out if they should be headbanging or practicing their best air violin? So, they brought in strings, horns, and all sorts of orchestral flair, and suddenly, The Move was transformed into Electric Light Orchestra.

Now, let's dissect that name. "Electric" implies energy, excitement, and perhaps a slight risk of electrocution if you're not careful. "Light" suggests brightness, positivity, and the kind of vibes you get from a sunny day at a music festival. And "Orchestra"? Well, that's just fancy. It's like they wanted to say, "We're not just a band; we're a full-blown musical experience!"

So here we are, left with a name that makes you feel like you're stepping into a concert hall, ready to groove while simultaneously marveling at the genius of orchestral rock. Who knew that a band almost named The Move would end up lighting up the music scene with a name that's both electrifying and delightfully whimsical?

Korn

You know, I've been doing some digging into the origins of one of the most iconic bands of the '90s, and let me tell you, the story behind their name is a wild ride. Picture this: a group of teenagers in Bakersfield, California, sitting around, probably eating too much pizza and discussing the meaning of life—or maybe just how to get through high school without losing their minds. They decide they want to start a band, and they know they need a name that's edgy, something that screams, "We're here to rock your socks off!" So, what do they come up with? Korn. Yes, Korn. But wait! It wasn't always Korn. Originally, they had a name that was even more ridiculous: Creep.

Now, Creep isn't bad, but it's also not exactly memorable. I mean, how many bands named Creep can you think of? Exactly. So, they brainstorm, and someone—probably after too many energy drinks—suggests "Korn." They thought it was funny to replace the C with a K because, you know, that's how you add a little edge to your name! It's like they were trying to spell "corn" but got distracted halfway through. And let's be honest, it's a name that sticks. You hear "Korn," and you know it's not some soft rock band that sings about love and rainbows. No, it's a band that's going to dive into the depths of angst and chaos.

So, next time you're rocking out to "Freak on a Leash" or "Got the Life," just remember: it all started with a couple of kids who thought "Creep" was too boring and decided to go with a name that sounds like a snack you'd find at a county fair. Who knew a simple twist of the alphabet could lead to a legacy?

INXS

Ah, INXS, the Australian rock band that took the world by storm in the late '80s and early '90s. But did you know that before they became the iconic INXS, they were known by a name that could only be described as a bad pun gone wild? Yes, their original name was "The Farriss Brothers," which sounds less like a rock band and more like a law firm specializing in personal injury cases. Can you imagine? "Injured? Call The Farriss Brothers! We'll get you the compensation you deserve!"

Now, don't get me wrong, the Farriss brothers—Andrew, Jon, and Kirk—were incredibly talented. But let's face it, that name lacked the punch of a good rock band. It was like calling a heavy metal group "The Gentlemen of Metal." It just doesn't scream "throw your hands in the air and rock out." So, in a stroke of genius—or perhaps sheer desperation—they decided to change their name.

They settled on INXS, which, let's be honest, sounds way cooler. It's mysterious, edgy, and rolls off the tongue like a rock anthem. But the real kicker? INXS stands for "in excess." You know, because they were all about living life to the fullest, partying hard, and cranking out hits like "Need You Tonight." It's a name that encapsulates their vibe perfectly.

Imagine if they had stuck with The Farriss Brothers. They'd be playing at family reunions instead of stadiums, and their biggest hit might have been a jingle for a local bakery. So, thank goodness for rebranding! INXS is a name that resonates, a name that makes you want to dance. And let's be real, who wouldn't want to rock out to a band with a name that sounds like it could be a secret code for an underground party?

Dire Straits

You know, it's funny how names can shape our perceptions, right? Take the band Dire Straits, for example. When you hear that name, you might picture a group of musicians struggling to make ends meet, desperately trying to pay the rent while living in a cramped flat. And honestly, that's not too far from the truth! But did you know that their original name was actually "Cafe Racers"? Yes, you heard me right! "Cafe Racers!" It sounds like a group of hipsters who would gather at a local diner, sipping artisanal coffee while debating the merits of vinyl records versus digital downloads. I can just imagine them, sporting leather jackets and slicked-back hair, strumming acoustic guitars while discussing the existential crisis of the modern musician.

But then, they decided to change it to Dire Straits, which, let's be real, sounds like a band that's one bad review away from being dropped by their label. It's like they wanted to set the bar low, just in case they needed an excuse for not hitting the big time. "Oh, we're in dire straits, you see? It's not us; it's the name!"

But here's the kicker: the name change was born out of necessity. They were literally in dire straits, struggling to find gigs and get noticed. So, they went from the whimsical "Cafe Racers" to a name that screamed, "Help! We need a hit!" And boy, did they get one! With hits like "Sultans of Swing," they went from struggling artists to rock legends. So, the next time you hear that name, remember it's not just a title; it's a testament to perseverance, desperation, and a dash of humor in the face of adversity. Who knew a name could carry such weight?

Guns N' Roses

You know, it's funny to think about how names can shape our perceptions, especially in the world of rock music. Take Guns N' Roses, for example. The legendary band that gave us anthems like "Sweet Child o' Mine" and "Welcome to the Jungle." But did you know they almost had a completely different name? Picture this: instead of the hard-hitting, rebellious vibe of Guns N' Roses, we could have been rocking out to a band called "Axl's Roses." I mean, can you imagine? Axl Rose strutting around on stage, flaunting a name that sounds more like a flower shop than a rock powerhouse? "Welcome to Axl's Roses, where the petals are as wild as our guitar solos!"

But it gets better. Before that, they briefly considered "The Axl Rose Band." Wow, what a stroke of genius! Nothing says "we're a team" quite like slapping the lead singer's name on the marquee. "Hey, everyone! Come see The Axl Rose Band! We've got one guy who's really good, and a bunch of others who are just happy to be here!" It's like naming a restaurant after yourself and then serving only your favorite dish. "Welcome to Chef Dave's Diner, where every meal is just a variation of mac and cheese!"

In the end, they settled on Guns N' Roses, a name that perfectly captures the duality of their sound: the hard edge of "Guns" and the softer, more melodic side of "Roses." It's a name that tells you to expect the unexpected, a wild ride through the highs and lows of rock 'n' roll. So next time you hear "Paradise City," just remember that it could have been playing in Axl's flower shop instead!

Soundgarden

You know, the origins of band names can be as weird as the bands themselves. Take Soundgarden, for example. They're one of the most iconic grunge bands to come out of Seattle, but their original name? Oh, it was a real head-scratcher. Before they settled on the moniker that would echo through the halls of rock history, they were briefly known as... wait for it... "The Shemps." Yes, you heard that right. The Shemps! It sounds like a group of guys who couldn't quite decide whether they wanted to be a rock band or a comedic troupe. I can just imagine them standing on stage, leather jackets and all, while the audience is left wondering if they'd come to see a concert or a slapstick comedy show.

Now, if you're scratching your head and thinking, "What in the world is a Shemp?" well, you're not alone. The name actually pays homage to Shemp Howard, one of the original Three Stooges. So, there you have it: a name that could have easily confused audiences into thinking they were about to hear a cover of "The Three Stooges Theme" instead of "Black Hole Sun."

But let's be honest, "The Shemps" sounds more like a band that would play at a county fair, right? Picture it: cotton candy, a Ferris wheel, and a bunch of guys in flannel trying to figure out how to play "Smells Like Teen Spirit" while the crowd is more interested in the pie-eating contest.

Eventually, they realized that they needed a name that reflected the darker, grungier vibe of their music. So, they went from Shemps to Soundgarden, and the rest is history. Thank goodness they made that switch; otherwise, we might be stuck singing "Shemps in the Rain" instead of "Black Hole Sun."

Linkin Park

You know, it's funny how names shape our perceptions, right? Take Linkin Park, for instance. You hear that name and you immediately think of angst, electric guitars, and maybe a little bit of nostalgia if you were a teenager in the early 2000s. But did you know they almost went by a completely different name? That's right! Before they became the iconic band we know and love, they were originally called Xero. Yes, Xero! Sounds like a failed tech startup, doesn't it? Picture a bunch of guys in a garage, surrounded by pizza boxes and energy drink cans, trying to figure out how to make a name that screams "we're here to rock your socks off!" And they land on Xero. I can just imagine the conversations: "Dude, what do you think of Xero?" "Uh, is that a band or a new flavor of yogurt?"

But it gets better. They changed their name to Hybrid Theory, which, let's be real, sounds like a college course on the evolution of rock music. I can see the syllabus now: "Week One: How to Blend Genres Without Losing Your Mind." But alas, that name was already taken, which led them to the final transformation into Linkin Park. Legend has it that the name was inspired by Lincoln Park in Santa Monica, but they had to tweak it a bit to secure the domain name. You know, because nothing says "we're serious musicians" like having a solid online presence in the late '90s.

So here we are, with Linkin Park, a name that's now synonymous with groundbreaking music. Who knew that a bunch of guys just trying to find their identity would end up creating a legacy? Xero to hero, am I right?

The Talking Heads

You know, it's funny how names can shape our perceptions. Take, for instance, the iconic band The Talking Heads. Now, you might think their name conjures images of deep philosophical discussions or maybe a quirky art installation, but in reality, it all started with something far more mundane. Originally, they were called The Artistics. Yes, The Artistics! Can you imagine? It sounds like a group of pretentious painters who only perform at gallery openings, sipping wine while dramatically reciting poetry about their feelings.

But let's be honest, "The Artistics" doesn't have the same punch, does it? It doesn't scream "we're going to revolutionize punk and new wave music!" It sounds more like a band you'd see at a coffeehouse, strumming acoustic guitars and lamenting about the existential dread of a Tuesday morning. I can picture it now: "Here's our next song, 'The Melancholy of Missing the Bus.'" Yawn!

Then, of course, there's the story of how they settled on The Talking Heads. Apparently, it was inspired by the phrase used in the media to describe people who were being interviewed on television. You know, those talking heads who just love to dispense their opinions like candy at a parade. It's the kind of name that suggests they're ready to engage in a lively debate about life, art, and why pineapple on pizza is a culinary crime.

So, thank goodness they ditched The Artistics for something as playful and evocative as The Talking Heads. It's a name that invites curiosity and a bit of humor, which is exactly what you want from a band that turned music into an art form—without the pretentiousness of an art gallery. Just a bunch of quirky, talented folks ready to make you think and dance at the same time. Now that's a win-win!

The Ramones

You know, the Ramones, those punk rock legends who practically defined a genre with their catchy riffs and three-chord anthems. But have you ever wondered what they were originally called? Picture this: it's the 1970s, New York City is buzzing with energy, and four guys from Queens are trying to make their mark on the music scene. They could have gone with something cool and edgy, but no, they chose to call themselves... wait for it... The Ramones! Oh, but that's not the whole story.

Before they settled on that iconic name, they toyed with the idea of calling themselves "The Ramones Brothers." Yes, you heard that right! It sounds like a family band that would play at your cousin's wedding, not the groundbreaking punk rock group we know today. Can you imagine? "The Ramones Brothers, live at CBGB!" The only thing they'd be breaking would be a few hearts with their cheesy ballads.

But it gets better. They were reportedly inspired by Paul McCartney, who used the pseudonym "Paul Ramone" when he checked into hotels. So, in a way, they were channeling their inner Beatle while trying to forge a path of their own. It's like they were saying, "Hey, we love the Beatles, but we want to be the rebellious little siblings who crash the party!"

In the end, they dropped the "Brothers" and embraced the simplicity of "The Ramones." And thank goodness they did, because "The Ramones" has a certain ring to it—like a battle cry for anyone who ever felt like they didn't fit in. So here's to the Ramones, the band that turned a name meant for family gatherings into an anthem for misfits everywhere!

The Stray Cats

You know, it's funny how names can stick with you, like that one friend who insists on calling you by your embarrassing childhood nickname, even though you've long since outgrown it. Take the rockabilly band The Stray Cats, for example. Most people think they just popped out of the womb with that slick name and cool vibe, but oh boy, were they in for a surprise! Originally, they were called The Tom Cats. Yes, you heard that right—The Tom Cats! Can you imagine? It's like naming a dog "Fido" when it clearly wants to be called "Rex."

Now, I get it. "Tom Cats" has that feline charm, but it sounds more like a local high school band playing at a sock hop than a group destined to rock the world. I mean, picture it: you're at a bar, and someone says, "Hey, did you catch The Tom Cats last night?" You'd probably think they were a tribute band for a cartoon or something. "Oh yes, they played all the hits from the '90s animated series!"

But The Stray Cats? That's a name that conjures up images of rebellious, leather-clad felines roaming the streets, looking for trouble and maybe a half-eaten slice of pizza. The shift from Tom to Stray was like going from a cute house pet to a wild, untamed creature that doesn't care about your rules. And let's be honest, it's a much better fit for a band that's all about that rockabilly lifestyle—swinging hips, slicked-back hair, and a whole lot of attitude.

So next time you're rocking out to "Stray Cat Strut," just remember: it could have been a lot worse. You could have been stuck with The Tom Cats, and that's a fate no one wants to face!

Black Flag

You know, when you think of iconic punk bands, Black Flag is right up there, with their aggressive sound and that unmistakable four-barred logo. But how many of you knew that they almost had a completely different name? That's right, the original name was... wait for it... Panic! Yes, Panic! Can you imagine? "Panic" is a name that conjures images of a group of teenagers running around screaming after a spider sighting or a dog chasing its tail. Not exactly the gritty, rebellious vibe we associate with Black Flag today.

So, let's break this down. The band formed in 1976 in Hermosa Beach, California, and they were all about pushing boundaries and challenging norms. But when they settled on "Panic," they probably didn't realize they were one bad hair day away from being mistaken for a pop band. I mean, how do you even market that? "Come see Panic! They're playing live at the local coffee shop!" It doesn't quite scream "mosh pit," does it?

Then, after some reflection, they decided to change their name to Black Flag. And thank goodness they did! Suddenly, they went from sounding like a bunch of kids with anxiety issues to a band that could take on the world. Black Flag evokes images of rebellion, resistance, and a certain level of chaos—perfect for a punk band.

So, here's a lesson for all you aspiring musicians out there: sometimes, names matter. You wouldn't want to be known as "Panic" when you could be "Black Flag." It's like choosing between a bowl of soggy cereal and a gourmet meal. One is just a mess, while the other is a full-on feast for the senses. So, here's to Black Flag—may their name forever strike fear into the hearts of the mainstream!

The New York Dolls

You know, when you think of rock bands that changed the landscape of music, The New York Dolls definitely come to mind. But did you know that their original name was actually "The Dolls"? I mean, it's like naming a dog "Dog." Sure, it's straightforward, but it lacks a certain pizzazz, right? Picture this: a bunch of glam rockers strutting around New York City in the early '70s, calling themselves just "The Dolls." It's almost like they were waiting for someone to say, "Hey, what's the name of your band?" and then they'd respond with a shrug, "Uh, we're The Dolls, but don't let that fool you. We're tough! Like, really tough! We can totally take you in a fight, just look at our eyeliner!"

But here's the kicker: the name "The Dolls" was already taken by a band that didn't quite make it. So, in a stroke of genius—or perhaps desperation—they tacked on "New York" to their name. Suddenly, they went from being a cute little plaything to a fierce, gritty representation of the city's rock scene. It's like they transformed from a dollhouse tea party to a full-blown punk rock riot!

Imagine the marketing meetings: "Okay, we need to stand out. How about we add 'New York'? It's edgy! It's urban! And who doesn't love a good city name?" It's the musical equivalent of adding "extra spicy" to a dish that was already too hot for most people to handle. And let's be honest, "The New York Dolls" just sounds cooler. It's got that ring to it, like a bell tolling for all the glam and chaos that was about to ensue. So, thank goodness they didn't stick with "The Dolls." Can you imagine? "Ladies and gentlemen, put your hands together for... The Dolls!" I don't think they would've gotten very far!

Tears For Fears

You know, it's funny how names can shape our perceptions of things. Take the rock band Tears For Fears, for instance. They've given us some of the most memorable anthems of the '80s, but did you know they almost went by a completely different name? Yes, indeed! Before they became the kings of emotional synth-pop, they were known as... wait for it... Graduate. Yes, Graduate! I mean, can you imagine? "Hey, did you hear the new Graduate song?" It sounds more like a graduation ceremony than a rock band, right? Picture it: a bunch of guys in caps and gowns strumming guitars while their parents cheer from the sidelines, tossing confetti that looks suspiciously like a mix of diploma paper and regret.

Now, the name Graduate was fitting, considering the band's early days. They were fresh out of school, full of youthful angst and existential dread, which is basically the fuel for all great music. But, let's be real, they needed a name that could encapsulate the emotional rollercoaster they were about to unleash on the world. Enter Tears For Fears. It's catchy, it's evocative, and it sounds like the title of a self-help book for people who cry during commercials.

The transformation from Graduate to Tears For Fears was like going from a high school science project to a full-blown rock opera. Suddenly, they weren't just a band; they were a phenomenon! They traded in their caps and gowns for leather jackets and synthesizers, and the rest is history. So, next time you're belting out "Everybody Wants to Rule the World," just remember, it could have been "Everybody Wants to Graduate." Now that's a thought that could make anyone shed a tear!

Mike and the Mechanics

You know, it's funny how names can shape our perceptions. Take, for instance, the band Mike and the Mechanics. Sounds pretty straightforward, doesn't it? Just a guy named Mike and his band of merry mechanics, ready to fix your musical woes. But, believe it or not, they almost had a completely different name that would have changed everything. Picture this: instead of Mike and the Mechanics, they could have been called Mike and the Mysterious Malfunctions! I mean, who wouldn't want to see that on a concert ticket?

Imagine the marketing! "Come see Mike and the Mysterious Malfunctions! They'll rock your socks off, or at least leave you wondering if your speakers are broken." The band could have leaned into it, creating a whole aesthetic of malfunctioning instruments, with guitars that spark and drums that occasionally just refuse to play. They could have had a mascot, like a cartoon wrench with sunglasses, leading the crowd in a chorus of "Oops, we did it again!"

But let's be real: the name Mike and the Mechanics has a certain charm. It evokes images of a reliable crew, the kind of guys you'd trust to fix your car or your broken heart with a catchy tune. The original name, though, would have set a different tone entirely. It would have been hard to take them seriously. "Oh, you're going to see Mike and the Mysterious Malfunctions? Good luck with that; I hear they might short-circuit halfway through the set!"

So here's to Mike and the Mechanics! They may not be mysterious, but they sure know how to deliver a hit. And who knows? Maybe their greatest malfunction was almost being stuck with a name that could've left audiences scratching their heads instead of tapping their feet.

Humble Pie

You know, when you think of classic rock bands, names like Led Zeppelin and The Rolling Stones come to mind, right? But have you ever stopped to consider the original name of Humble Pie? Yes, Humble Pie! A name that evokes images of wholesome family dinners, not exactly the gritty, rebellious vibe you'd expect from a rock band. But here's the kicker: they weren't always called Humble Pie. No, no, no! They were initially known as... wait for it... "Humble Pie and the Munchkins." Yes, you heard that right! The Munchkins! It sounds like a children's band performing at a birthday party, not a rock group that would eventually give us hits like "30 Days in the Hole."

Can you imagine? Picture it: a bunch of leather-clad rockers on stage, belting out tunes while a bunch of little kids in colorful outfits dance around them. It's like a bizarre mashup of "The Wizard of Oz" and a rock concert, and frankly, I'm not sure how they thought that name would work. I mean, were they planning on throwing in some whimsical choreography? "Hey, let's rock out to our next song while doing the Hokey Pokey!" I can see the headlines: "Humble Pie and the Munchkins: The Most Confusing Concert of the Year!"

Eventually, they realized that the name didn't quite capture their essence. So, they dropped the Munchkins and settled on Humble Pie, which sounds a lot more serious, like they're ready to take on the world with a side of humility. But let's be honest, every time I hear their name, I can't help but think of dessert. Rock and roll? More like rock and pie! So next time you jam out to Humble Pie, just remember: it could have been a whole different musical experience if they'd stuck with the Munchkins!

Coldplay

You know, it's funny how names can shape our perceptions. Take Coldplay, for instance. When you hear the name, you might think of ethereal melodies, introspective lyrics, and a whole lot of heartfelt ballads. But did you know that before they were Coldplay, they were called... wait for it... Pectoralz? Yes, Pectoralz! Can you imagine that? I mean, it sounds like a supplement you'd take before hitting the gym, or maybe a fancy new protein shake. "Hey guys, I just chugged some Pectoralz! Let's rock out!"

The band members, bless their hearts, were probably thinking they were the next big thing, flexing their musical muscles with a name like that. But let's be real: who would want to buy a ticket to see Pectoralz live? You'd expect a bunch of guys in tank tops flexing their biceps while belting out tunes about protein shakes and the importance of leg day.

Eventually, they realized that Pectoralz wasn't going to get them very far, so they rebranded. They came up with the name Coldplay, which, let's face it, sounds much cooler and more sophisticated. It evokes images of snowy landscapes and deep emotions, rather than a sweaty gym session.

And the best part? The name change didn't just save their reputation; it also gave us some of the most iconic songs of the early 2000s. So, thank you, universe, for steering them away from Pectoralz. I mean, can you imagine the headlines? "Pectoralz releases new album, gains 10 pounds in the process!"

So the next time you find yourself humming "Yellow" or "Fix You," just remember: it could have been a whole lot worse. You could have been stuck with a band named after a gym routine!

Megadeth

You know, when you think of iconic rock bands, names like Metallica, Slayer, and of course, Megadeth come to mind. But did you know that before they settled on the name Megadeth, they toyed with something completely different? Picture this: a group of young musicians, fueled by ambition and maybe a little too much caffeine, gathered in a garage somewhere, trying to find the perfect name that screamed "we're heavy metal and we mean business!" So, what did they come up with? "Fallen Angels." Yes, you heard that right. Fallen Angels. It sounds more like a failed boy band than a thrash metal powerhouse, doesn't it? I can almost see the marketing team struggling to sell T-shirts with that name. "Hey, Mom! Can I get a Fallen Angels hoodie for Christmas?"

But here's the kicker: the name was inspired by a mix of biblical references and a desire to sound edgy. I mean, who doesn't want to channel their inner angelic rebellion? But, as fate would have it, they realized it was as forgettable as a one-hit wonder from the '80s. So, they went back to the drawing board, which is where the genius of Dave Mustaine came into play. He had an epiphany—an actual epiphany!—about the concept of "megadeath," a term he coined that refers to the death of one million people, often used in the context of nuclear warfare. Talk about a mood shift!

So, they transformed from Fallen Angels to Megadeth, and the rest is history. Who wouldn't want to rock out to a name that sounds like a nuclear explosion, right? It's the perfect blend of chaos and creativity, proving that sometimes, the best names are born from a little bit of insanity and a whole lot of rock 'n' roll!

Butthole Surfers

So, let's take a moment to dive into the wonderfully bizarre world of rock band names, specifically the legendary Butthole Surfers. Now, you might think, "What a name! How did they come up with that?" Well, believe it or not, they didn't start with that gem. The original name for this eclectic group was actually "The Butthole Surfers." Yes, you heard that right, they were going for something a little less refined but still equally absurd.

Imagine a bunch of guys in Texas, sitting around, probably high on something unidentifiable, and thinking, "You know what would really sell? A name that sounds like it came straight out of a middle school locker room!" And voilà, the Butthole Surfers were born. But before that, they toyed with names like "The Shit Dogs" and "The Big Boys." Honestly, it's like they were playing a game of 'how ridiculous can we get?' They were practically daring the music industry to take them seriously.

Now, the beauty of their name lies in its sheer audacity. It's the kind of name that makes your mom gasp and your dad chuckle, all while you're trying to explain to your friends that yes, they are a real band and no, you can't just make up names like that. They embraced the absurd, and their music reflected that chaos.

But here's the kicker: the Butthole Surfers weren't just about shock value. They were pioneers of combining punk, psychedelic rock, and performance art, all while sporting a name that could make a nun blush. So next time you hear their music, remember, behind that outrageous name is a band that didn't just want to rock your world; they wanted to make you laugh, think, and maybe cringe just a little.

The Cramps

You know, when we think about iconic rock bands, names like The Beatles, The Rolling Stones, or even Nirvana come to mind, right? But let's talk about The Cramps for a second. Now, this band is legendary, known for their wild blend of punk rock and rockabilly, but did you know they almost had a completely different name? Picture this: a band that could have been known as The Cramps... or The Cramps of the Universe! Okay, maybe not that dramatic, but they did start off with a name that might make you chuckle. They were originally called The Cramps of the Universe, which sounds like a bad sci-fi novel from the '70s, right? Can you imagine them on stage, rocking out with that name? "Ladies and gentlemen, welcome to the intergalactic sounds of The Cramps of the Universe!" It's like they were trying to channel their inner cosmic rock gods while simultaneously sounding like they might sell you a used spaceship afterward.

But wait, it gets better. The name change to just The Cramps came about because, let's be honest, who wants to lug around the entire universe on their band t-shirts? I mean, have you tried fitting that on a marquee? It's a logistical nightmare! Plus, think about the poor merchandise guy. "Hey, can I get a dozen shirts in size medium?" "Sure, which universe?"

In the end, The Cramps became a household name, but I can't help but wonder what would have happened if they had stuck with that original title. Would they have had a cult following of space enthusiasts? Would they have collaborated with aliens? Who knows!

But one thing's for sure: The Cramps of the Universe would have been a tough act to follow!

The Psychedelic Furs

You know, it's funny how names can shape perceptions. Take, for instance, the original name of the iconic band, the Psychedelic Furs. Before they became synonymous with post-punk coolness, they were briefly known as "Rugby." Yes, Rugby! Can you imagine? A name that conjures images of a bunch of blokes in mismatched jerseys tackling each other on a muddy field, rather than the moody, atmospheric soundscapes we associate with their music today.

Picture it: "Hey, have you heard Rugby's new single?" It just doesn't pack the same punch, does it? I mean, who would take a band called Rugby seriously? It sounds like a group of guys who'd rather be passing a ball than passing the mic. The name evokes a sense of camaraderie, sure, but also a distinct lack of edge. It's like calling a rock band "The Fluffy Kittens" and expecting them to headline a festival.

But then they made the leap to Psychedelic Furs, and suddenly, everything changed. The name evokes a sense of mystery, a hint of rebellion, and a dash of the avant-garde. It's like they went from a weekend rugby match to an underground rave, complete with neon lights and a haze of smoke. And let's be honest, who doesn't want to be part of something that sounds like it might involve a little bit of mind expansion?

So, here's to the Psychedelic Furs, who traded in the scrappy charm of Rugby for something that truly reflects their sound. It's a reminder that sometimes, a name can be everything. Just imagine if they'd stuck with Rugby. We'd all be missing out on some seriously great tunes and a whole lot of coolness. So, next time you think about band names, remember: it's not just a label; it's your entire vibe!

Foo Fighters

YOU KNOW, IT'S FUNNY how names can shape our perceptions, especially when it comes to rock bands. Take, for example, the band we all know and love today as the Foo Fighters. But did you know that their original name was actually "The Dee Gees"? Yes, you heard that right! It sounds like a group of disco-loving, polyester-wearing enthusiasts ready to boogie down, not a powerhouse rock band that has given us anthems to scream along to. Can you imagine? "Hey, let's crank up 'Everlong' by The Dee Gees!" It's like inviting your friends over for a night of headbanging and ending up with a dance-off in your living room instead.

Now, the name change came about because, well, "The Dee Gees" was a bit of a joke. It was a playful nod to the band's roots in the grunge scene, and perhaps a wink at the Bee Gees, those disco legends. But when you're trying to carve out a legacy in rock 'n' roll, you need something that packs a punch, not a fluffy Saturday Night Fever vibe. So, in a moment of genius—or perhaps desperation—Dave Grohl and the gang decided that a name change was in order. They needed something that would resonate with the fans, something that would make you think of UFOs, secret military projects, and all things mysterious. Enter "Foo Fighters," a name inspired by World War II slang for unidentified flying objects.

Suddenly, they went from being the disco darlings of the Dee Gees to rock titans of the Foo Fighters. Who knew a name could make such a difference? So next time you're rocking out, remember: it could have been a whole lot of polyester and glitter instead!

Judas Priest

You know, it's funny how some things just stick with us, like that one song you can't get out of your head or the name of a band that's become iconic. But did you know that the legendary heavy metal band Judas Priest almost had a completely different name? Picture this: it's the early 1970s, and a group of guys in England are trying to figure out what to call themselves. They toss around all sorts of wild ideas, but nothing seems to stick. Then, out of nowhere, they come up with "The Flying Hat Band." Yes, you heard that right. The Flying Hat Band! Can you imagine? I mean, what were they thinking? Was there a particularly impressive hat involved? Maybe it was an oversized sombrero that just soared through the air, or perhaps a wizard's hat that granted them musical powers.

But then again, who wouldn't want to see a band with a name like that? It sounds like they'd be opening for a circus act, juggling flaming swords while belting out power ballads. But thankfully, they soon realized that the name didn't quite capture the essence of their music. So, they scrapped it and went for something a bit more menacing. Enter Judas Priest, a name that conjures images of leather, spikes, and a whole lot of headbanging.

Now, the name Judas Priest has become synonymous with heavy metal, but it's hard not to chuckle at the thought of them rocking out as The Flying Hat Band. Can you picture the album covers? "Flying Hats Over England," or "The Hat's Revenge"? It's a reminder that sometimes, the road to greatness is paved with ridiculousness. So here's to Judas Priest and their epic evolution from flying hats to heavy metal legends!

The Scorpions

Imagine a world where one of the most iconic rock bands in history was not known as The Scorpions but instead carried a name that sounded more like a bad B-movie or a questionable high school mascot. Yes, I'm talking about the original name of the band: The Scorpions were initially called The Nameless Band. Yes, you heard that right. The Nameless Band! It's like they were trying to win an award for the most forgettable band name in history. Picture it: the lights dim, the crowd buzzes with anticipation, and then—"Ladies and gentlemen, please welcome... The Nameless Band!" Cue the crickets. Who would want to buy a T-shirt from a band that doesn't even know what to call itself?

Now, you might think, "What were they thinking?" Well, it turns out, they were probably just as confused as we are. Maybe they thought it would be mysterious, like a magician who never reveals his secrets. Or perhaps they were waiting for inspiration to strike, like a bolt of lightning, which, ironically, is what they needed to electrify their image.

But then, like a scorpion that sheds its skin, they transformed into The Scorpions, a name that conjures images of danger, allure, and a hint of rock 'n' roll rebellion. Suddenly, they went from being the band that might play at your cousin's wedding to the band that would headline at stadiums, commanding the attention of thousands.

So, next time you crank up "Rock You Like a Hurricane," just remember, it could have been a lot worse. We could have been rocking out to The Nameless Band! And honestly, who wants to explain that to their friends? "Hey, have you heard the latest from The Nameless Band?" Yeah, no thanks.

The Beach Boys

You know, there's a little nugget of rock history that never fails to crack me up every time I think about it. The Beach Boys, those sun-soaked, surf-loving legends of the '60s, didn't always go by that iconic name. Nope! They were originally known as The Pendletones. Yes, you heard that right! The Pendletones, like a group of plaid-clad lumberjacks who just stumbled off a mountain and decided to form a band. I can't help but imagine them in those thick wool shirts, strumming their guitars while trying to figure out how to surf on land.

The name was inspired by the Pendleton wool shirts that were all the rage back then. You know, the kind that made you look like you were about to chop wood or start a campfire. I mean, can you picture them? "Hey, let's name our band after these cozy shirts!" It's almost as if they were trying to sell a line of flannel fashion rather than create timeless music.

But here's where it gets even better. When they recorded their first single, "Surfin'," the record label thought Pendletones sounded a bit too much like a knitting club. So, they decided to change it to The Beach Boys. Talk about a glow-up! From lumberjack chic to surfboard dreams! The name change was like swapping a pair of heavy boots for flip-flops. Suddenly, they were riding the waves of pop culture instead of just sitting around a campfire.

So, the next time you hear "Good Vibrations" or "California Girls," just remember: behind those harmonies was a band that almost had us all thinking they were the world's first musical woodchoppers. The

Beach Boys? More like The Pendletones, the most laid-back lumberjack band you never knew you needed!

The Tubes

Imagine a time when rock music was still finding its feet, a time when bands were named after all sorts of oddities and whims. The Tubes, a band that would later become known for their outrageous performances and eclectic sound, originally had a name that could make you scratch your head in confusion. They were first called "The Beans." Yes, you heard that right—The Beans! Now, I don't know about you, but when I think of rock 'n' roll, I don't picture a can of baked beans sitting in my pantry. I mean, what's next? The Peas? The Carrots? The Corn? It's a culinary nightmare waiting to happen!

The story goes that the band members were just a bunch of kids in San Francisco, trying to make a name for themselves in the music scene. They were young, energetic, and apparently had a fondness for legumes. Maybe they thought it would be catchy, or perhaps they just really loved beans. Who knows? But as their music evolved, so did their name. They realized that "The Beans" didn't quite capture the essence of their theatricality and innovative sound. So, they decided to rebrand themselves, and what better way to do that than to name themselves after a tube?

But wait—what kind of tube? A toothpaste tube? A tube of paint? The possibilities are endless! They finally settled on "The Tubes," which not only sounded cooler but also hinted at their flamboyant performances and the various mediums they used to express their art. So, next time you rock out to "She's a Beauty," just remember: it all started with a name that was more suitable for a grocery list than a rock band. And that, my friends, is the deliciously absurd origin of The Tubes!

Radiohead

YOU KNOW, IT'S FUNNY how some of the biggest names in music started off with names that sound like they were pulled from a hat at a middle school talent show. Take Radiohead, for instance. Yes, the band that gave us "Creep" and "Karma Police" was not always known by that iconic moniker. Originally, they went by the name "On a Friday." I mean, can you imagine? "On a Friday" sounds more like a mediocre sitcom than a groundbreaking band. "Hey, did you catch the latest episode of On a Friday? They really nailed that awkward family dinner scene!"

The name was a product of their early days, when they were just a bunch of teenagers jamming in a garage, dreaming of rock stardom while trying to figure out how to play their instruments without breaking too many strings or their parents' patience. It's like they were trying to capture the essence of casualness, as if they were just a bunch of friends hanging out, trying to figure out what to do with their weekend. Spoiler alert: they ended up changing their name, and thankfully so!

When they signed with a record label, they realized "On a Friday" wasn't going to cut it. It lacked the punch, the intrigue, the "Hey, we're going to change the world with our music" vibe. So, they opted for Radiohead, inspired by a Talking Heads song. Suddenly, they went from sounding like the band you'd see playing at your local coffee shop to one that would headline Glastonbury. Who knew a name change could be so transformative? So here's to Radiohead, the band that proves sometimes all it takes to go from garage band to legends is a better name and a lot of talent. Cheers to that!

Oingo Boingo

You know, it's funny how names can shape our perception of things, like how a name can make a band sound cool or utterly ridiculous. Take Oingo Boingo, for instance. You hear that name, and it's like a burst of confetti in your brain—colorful, chaotic, and slightly confusing. But did you know that before they were the beloved band we know today, they had a name that sounded like it was pulled from a children's book? That's right! They originally called themselves the Mystic Knights of the Oingo Boingo. I mean, come on! That sounds like a Dungeons & Dragons campaign gone wrong. Picture a bunch of guys in capes, wielding imaginary swords, and trying to convince you that their music is the soundtrack to your next epic quest.

The Mystic Knights were more than a band; they were a theatrical experience. They wore costumes, performed skits, and probably had a lot of fun convincing audiences that they were the coolest knights in town. But let's be honest, who wants to scream "I'm going to see the Mystic Knights of the Oingo Boingo!" at a concert? You'd sound like you were announcing your plans to join a medieval reenactment group.

So, they trimmed it down to Oingo Boingo, which sounds like a quirky carnival ride—something that spins you around and leaves you feeling dizzy but exhilarated. And let's not forget the irony! They became a staple of the 80s music scene, with hits like "Weird Science" and "Dead Man's Party." Who knew that behind that silly name was a band that would capture the essence of a generation? So next time you hear Oingo Boingo, just remember: it all started with a bunch of Mystic Knights trying to rock the world, one bizarre name at a time.

Badfinger

You know, it's funny how names can stick with us, like that one awkward nickname from high school that just won't die. Take the rock band Badfinger, for example. When you think of them, you probably picture catchy tunes and a legacy that's intertwined with some of the biggest names in music history. But did you know they started out with a name that sounds more like a bad joke than a legendary band? They were originally called The Iveys. Yes, The Iveys! Can you imagine that? It sounds like a group of overly enthusiastic botanists who decided to form a band during their lunch breaks at the local greenhouse. "Hey, everyone! Let's play some tunes about photosynthesis!"

The name change came about when they signed with Apple Records, the label founded by none other than The Beatles. And you know how it is when you're trying to impress the cool kids—suddenly, The Iveys just didn't cut it. They needed something edgier, something that screamed rock and roll. So, they chose Badfinger, inspired by a working title for a Beatles song. It's almost poetic, isn't it? A name born from the very essence of the music they idolized, but with a twist that makes it sound like a band that might show up at your local dive bar to play a set of covers and then challenge you to a game of darts.

But let's be real, Badfinger is a name that sticks. It's memorable, it's quirky, and it's a reminder that sometimes, the best things in life come from the most unexpected places—even if that place involves a finger that's, well, a little bad. So here's to Badfinger, the band that took a botanical name and turned it into rock history, one catchy tune at a time!

Bay City Rollers

You know, when you think of the Bay City Rollers, you probably picture plaid pants, catchy tunes, and a whole lot of teenage hysteria. But did you know that their original name was... wait for it... the "Sandy Denny Band"? I know, right? It sounds like a folk group that would perform at an artsy coffee shop, sipping herbal tea and discussing the meaning of life between songs. Imagine the confusion when they showed up at a stadium packed with screaming fans expecting a rock concert!

Now, let's break this down. Sandy Denny, for those who don't know, was a brilliant British folk singer. So, to name a band after her was a bold move, but let's face it, it lacked the pizzazz that a group with a future as bright as theirs required. They soon realized that if they wanted to capture the hearts of the youth, they needed something that screamed "fun" and "party"—not "let's sit in a circle and share our feelings."

Enter the Bay City Rollers! The name itself is like a rollercoaster ride—exciting, full of twists and turns, and just a bit nauseating if you go too fast. And let's not forget the "Bay City" part. It conjures images of sun-soaked beaches and carefree summer days, which is far more appealing than a band named after a folk singer who probably spent her weekends knitting and contemplating existential dread.

So, there you have it. From the Sandy Denny Band to the Bay City Rollers, it's a classic case of rebranding gone right. Who knew that a name could make such a difference? I mean, would you rather roll with the Bay City Rollers or sit around with Sandy Denny and her knitting circle? I think we all know the answer to that one!

The Yardbirds

You know, there's a quirky little tidbit about one of rock's most legendary bands, The Yardbirds, that always tickles me. Originally, they weren't known as The Yardbirds at all. Nope! They started out as The Metropolis Blues Quartet. I mean, can you imagine that? The Metropolis Blues Quartet! It sounds like a jazz group that would serenade you while you sip overpriced coffee in a hipster café, not the band that would go on to influence the likes of Eric Clapton, Jimmy Page, and Jeff Beck.

Picture it: a bunch of guys in matching turtlenecks, playing smooth blues tunes, and talking about existential angst in a smoky basement. I can just hear them now, "Hey man, let's take this blues thing and really... make it a quartet." I mean, who knew that the path to rock royalty would start with such a bland name?

But then, the band realized that "Metropolis Blues Quartet" lacked a certain punch. It didn't quite scream "let's rock out" or "we're going to change the face of music." So, they decided to rebrand themselves. They tossed around a few ideas, and eventually, they landed on The Yardbirds. Now that's a name that sticks! It conjures up images of raucous energy, and maybe even a few drunken backyard parties.

The story goes that the name "Yardbirds" was inspired by a slang term for "a person who spends time in the yard"—you know, a bit of a slacker. Ironically, these so-called "slackers" went on to become rock legends. So, the next time you hear "For Your Love" or "Heart Full of Soul," just remember: it all started with a name that would have definitely been more at home in a coffee shop than on a stadium stage.

The Hollies

You know, it's funny how names can shape a band's identity, right? Take The Hollies, for instance. I mean, when you hear that name, you might picture a bunch of cheerful lads, strumming guitars in a sunlit park, singing about love and good times. But did you know that their original name was... wait for it... The Fourteen Iced Bears? Yes, you heard me correctly! Fourteen Iced Bears! I can only assume they were trying to channel some sort of quirky Arctic vibe, perhaps thinking that the frigid imagery would attract a cooler crowd.

Imagine the confusion at their gigs! "Hey, we're The Fourteen Iced Bears!" And the audience would be like, "Are we supposed to bring the honey? Because I'm not sure how this works!" I mean, who wants to be known as a band that sounds like a failed children's cartoon? It's hard to take a group seriously when they sound like they're about to launch a line of plush toys.

But then, they decided to switch things up. They went from frosty bears to The Hollies, inspired by the legendary Buddy Holly. A much more sensible choice, right? Suddenly, they went from being a frozen novelty act to a band that could actually rock out and be taken seriously.

And let's be honest, The Hollies has a nice ring to it. It's catchy, it's memorable, and it doesn't conjure up images of polar bear picnics. Just think of all the classic hits we'd have missed if they'd stuck with that original name. "He Ain't Heavy, He's My Fourteen Iced Bear" doesn't quite have the same emotional punch, does it? So here's to The Hollies, the band that learned that sometimes, less is more—even if it means leaving the bears out in the cold!

The Who

So, let's take a trip back in time to the early 1960s, a decade filled with bell-bottoms, psychedelic colors, and music that could make you feel like you were floating on a cloud of happiness—unless, of course, you were trying to come up with a band name. Enter The Who, one of the most iconic rock bands in history, but did you know they didn't start off as The Who? Oh no, my friends, they originally went by the name The Detours. Yes, The Detours! And what a name that was—perfectly pedestrian, like a pair of sensible shoes at a rock concert.

Imagine the scene: a bunch of young lads, all eager to take the music world by storm, but their name sounds like they were just trying to find their way to the nearest bus stop. "Hey, are you going to see The Detours tonight?" "Sure! I'll just take a detour on my way to the good band!"

But wait, it gets better. They were also briefly known as The High Numbers, which sounds like a group of accountants who decided to take up music as a hobby. "We're The High Numbers, and we're here to rock your spreadsheets!"

Finally, they settled on The Who, a name that still makes people scratch their heads. I mean, it's a question! "Who?" It's like they were inviting everyone to join in on a cosmic game of charades. "Who's on stage?" "I don't know, who?" "Exactly!"

So there you have it, folks. From The Detours to The High Numbers, and then to The Who, a journey that proves sometimes you just have to embrace the absurdity of it all. Because in the end, it's not about the name; it's about the music, and boy, did they make some unforgettable tunes!

Also by Michael Pollick

Michael Pollick's Proving Ground
Michael Pollick's Proving Ground
The Keepinnit Reels
The Keepinnit Reels 2: Acoustic Boogaloo
The Zero Sugar Keepinnit Reels
Professor Mike's Low-Flow Fountain Of Information
A Wise Geek's Guide To Everything
A Wise Geek's Guide To Everything Volume 2
Professor Mike's Wealth Of Geeky Knowledge
Casting Conquests: The Surprising Runner-Ups for Iconic Roles
Avoiding the Disaster Date: Funny But True Stories of Relationship
Red Flags
The Keepinnit Reels 3: Revenge Or Return Of The Snark
The Name Game: Forgotten Names of Legendary Rock Groups

www.ingramcontent.com/pod-product-compliance
Lightning Source LLC
Chambersburg PA
CBHW061454150726
47987CB00001B/442